What people from around the world have to say

As in BODY LANGUAGE, we know that the game of life has a set of rules and blue print. Successful people have learned and mastered the rules of the game. THE BOOK on Winning The Game Of Life is your opportunity to learn and apply the blue print to success.

Allan and Barbara Pease International authors of
#1 best-selling book - The Definitive Book of Body Language
http://www.peaseinternational.com/

"If you would just read pages 37 - 45, 'Letting it happen vs Making it happen', then you'll know this book is for you. Why didn't someone tell us this in high school?"

Tom BIG AL Schreiter- Leading Network Marketing Expert - America
- www.fortunenow.com

"Great common sense advice of success from someone who did it himself and can help you do it too! Pay close attention, apply the principles, and enjoy the rewards!"

Chris Widener, NY Times Best-selling Author of The Angel Inside
http://www.chriswidener.com/

"Amazingly insightful, Kevin has managed to write a book that actually teaches people how to really be successful. I recommend hands down Winning The Game Of Life to anyone committed to make it."

Nordine Zouareg -International Celebrity Fitness Coach and Author of
Mind Over Body: The Key To Lasting Weight Loss Is All In Your Head!-
http://www.nordinez.com/

"Study This Book As If Your Life Depended On I
Darren Jacklin - MEGA MANIFESTOR-
http://www.darrenjacklin.com

Kevin's book is essential reading for anyone interested in moving closer to their dreams. If you want to read a simple, open and honest book on what separates success from failure, then make it this one!

Farzan Athari- International Model- www.FarzanAthari.com

As in all of my books, Kevin has not only written the secrets to success, but they are things he has not just written, but things he has done. Success happens when you follow in the footsteps of other successful people. You cannot earn more than you learn, get learning … Enjoy the read …

Bradley J Sugars, Author of the Business Coach and CEO of ActionCoach

"Winning the Game of Life is a practical and inspiring book written with wit and wisdom!"

Azim Jamal, # 1 Amazon bestselling co-author of "The Power of Giving"

Kevin's writings! - Simply amazing! No words would exactly describe. Voila in the words of Prof. Ed Morato, author of strategic management and self mastery. The words are powerfully executed that you will feel it running in your veins! Exactly said by Kevin.

Aleem Guiapal, Member of the Board of Directors, Asian Institute of Management Student Association – Philippines

"In The Book on Winning the Game of Life, Kevin Abdulrahman packs a lot of power in its pages. He gives the reader a heartfelt reminder to stand up and embrace the life that you want, and he does this the only way he can, through sharing his story, his experience. The tried and true science of successful living is brought to light as the pages encourage you to value results over mere effort and to move with the passion and desire toward your perfect vision. Read this book and read it again, do the exercises. It will spur you to take action and overcome self-imposed limitations, and you will never look back "

Steve Cotter, internationally renowned pioneer of mind-body fitness www.fullkontact.com

This book is incredible for anyone who wants to be the best they can be and to unleash the wonderful power they have already within them. The excercises, tools and wonderful strength the words give you all let you go forward with your dreams and let you reach your ptoential. I definite must read.

Lucinda Ruh, Figure skating champion and Guinness world record holder for the Fastest and longest spinner on ice in the world www.lucindaruh.com

"Kevin Abdulrahman's book is the work of someone who had every reason to lie around waiting for the world to deliver his dreams. He just did one thing different to most of us. He consistently took massive action. To get you focused on your way I suggest you read this and start livingthe way you desire to".

Mike Handcock - Founder of Rock Your Life - New Zealand- www.rockyourlife.net

"Sound advice and a simple message for any young person who wanted to identify their purpose in life and achieve exceptional results."

John J. Scott.- Organisational Development Manager- United Kingdom

I am going through your book. Its really interesting and today's life its necessary for all to read this book. The book is really interesting and in today's life, it's necessary for all to read this book.

Chithra Kannan- India

"Are you stuck and don't know why? Do you long for more in life but don't know how to get it? If you've answered "yes", THE BOOK™ is exactly what you need…NOW. Filled with an entertaining blend of humour and sincerity, Kevin Abdulrahman reveals the secrets to winning the game of life."

Gina Fink-Bell - co-Founder of The Networking Masters- www.TheNetworkingMasters.com

"Take time now to read Kevin's book. Follow the activities and plans inside to help you build and live out your dreams. You can make a positive difference in your life today. As Kevin says in the book, "Plan, execute, and CONQUER." I highly recommend this book.

Cordell Jones - Business Marketing Expert and Trainer

"Kevin exposes "Opinions" in this Glowing and Brilliant read. If you would follow pages 65-69 you may be one step closer to your emotional success, which in turn, would lead you to your financial success. Allow Kevin's finesse to inspire you through this book."

Hillary B. Patz - Leading Internet Marketer- Shorewood, WI USA

"Kevin's enthusiasm jumps off the page, grabs you by the scruff of the neck and yanks you into a turbocharged state of desire and optimism. Lots of great visual tools to connect where you are to where you want to be. A great book for getting off the fence and into inspired action."

Larry Hochman, M.S., C.A.G.S. - Author, Juggler, Trainer and Facilitator of Dreams Fulfilled - USA - www.NoMoreHoldingBack.com

Kevin guides you to a profound level of inspiration and understanding on the principals of achieving success like no other book has done before.

The infinite doors of opportunities open as he expands your mind and sets you in creative action to Winning the Game of Life.

Alida Fehily, Mysteries of Wisdom, Wisdom Consultant, Australia - www.alidafehily.com.au

Kevin Abdulrahman is simply brilliant; he has assembled THE SECRET WEAPONS that is utilized by successful people to reach great heights. I found THE BOOK on Winning The Game Of Life to be not just helpful but practical, thus, it's an essential tool in order to win the most important game you'll ever play, life. If you want to start living the life that you dream about instead of wondering how it is possible grab a copy of Kevin's book now, he has done the research and now you can reap the benefits too.

Nicolette Jackson- Entrepreneur - St. Vincent and the Grenadines, W. I.

"Winning The Game Of Life is one of those rare books that once you've read it, you want to share it with everyone you know. Many people have influenced me in various ways for various reasons. My parents (so many ways), Ayn Rand (philosophy), Jackson Pollock (painting), Jay Abraham (marketing) and now Kevin Abdulrahman. I've only known Kevin for a short time but his ideas, his outlook and his way of seeing the world have already influenced me. I'm not only a fan, but also proud to call Kevin a friend."

Marti Garaughty-The Blog Artist- http://garaughty.com

"Kevin sheds light on the foggy road we often find ourselves on. The exercises at the end of each chapter help to reinforce his message and put the reader on a straight forward path to successful thinking and being... I found myself having little ah ha moments throughout the book"

Melissa Ward, Managing Partner, New Ward Development LLC - www.newward.com

Part time I sell wine in a call centre and I'm not financially free and super successful...YET! however with the wisdom found in Kevin's book I am definitely well on my way as the secrets revealed are very insightful, helpful and very simple to apply in real life. I've found that all one needs to do is to 'just do' what the book says and progress will be noticed instantaneously.

The chapters are very easy to understand with excellent examples relating to real life situations anyone and everyone should find majorly helpful in at least one way or another. Thank you Kevin, not just for the great book, but for the constant example you set for all of us.

Waan Huynh- University student/salesperson studying politics, philosopy, and sales- Auckland

"Winning the Game of Life" is a wonderful book that you won't be able to put down. If you are ready to change your life and move ahead a lightening-speed this is a must read."

Debbie Allen, International business speaker and best selling author of "Confessions of Shameless Self Promoters"

"There are a lot of wealth in people but few that are willing to share their knowledge so freely. Congratulations Kevin for a marvellous book. It is packed with useable information and leaves you feeling inspired to embark on your own success journey."

Dale Beaumont- Author of 16 books and Creator of the Secrets Exposed Club- Australia http://www.SecretsExposedClub.com

I recommend this to anyone looking to change their lives for the better. This is powerful stuff and should not be missed by anyone. All the best...

Ben Hulme- United Kingdom – http://www.PlatinumRights.com

Sometimes we can be so busy these days and totally distracted. Who has the time available to ponder upon anything more than what is immediately in front of us? We get so focused on what we plan to eat for breakfast this morning, what clothes am I going to wear today? Have I sorted out the recycling? So at first glance reading any self improvement book to the end can seem daunting. This is not so when you read Kevin's new book "Winning the Game of Life". You will see how quick, easy and very enjoyable a read his book is. I remember meeting Kevin briefly over 4 years ago, and he still remembered me today, right to the exact instance of where I was at in my life. Kevin is a Great Guy! And his book is the perfect read for people who want to win their own game. There are a number of strategies and tactics that I have personally taken out of the book from, Dealing with failure, How to model others success, and that being a Dreamer is a good thing! I highly recommend you read "Winning the Game of Life". Just grab a hot drink, jump on the couch and you will be able read it in one afternoon.

Matthew Taylor- Professional Poker Player- Australia

"This book has a golden key that will open the door to a new life; a life in which you can actually have it all. Kevin keeps it simple and fun!"

Karen Hoyos- Global Transformational Leader- www.karenhoyos.com

"If you want to make a change in your life this book will give you the initial tools and strategies you need to get the wheels on motion. Kevin style is simple & informal yet fun and insightful. This book can also be used as a tool to evaluate your current "success rating". I highly recommend reading this book to success searching beginners and to experienced achievers alike."

David Leon - Author, entrepreneur & Acclaimed international speaker- www.davidleon.biz

"If you are looking for some direction or steps to success this book is a brilliant blue print, and a great way to 'snap yourself back into success'"

Pete Williams (Entrepreneur, Australia)

All my life I have been a dreamer. Even though it all seemed so far fetched, I wanted to be a singer, I wanted to be a Television Entertainer but once that was achieved I wondered "where to now?" I almost listened to those who said it stops there but Kevin's book Winning the Game of Life has helped me realize that it doesn't stop there. In fact now more than ever I look forward to what lies ahead. So I urge you too to read the book, but most importantly APPLY it.

Megan Alatini- Television Icon

It is rare to come across a book that has great content followed by practical exercises that are 'in your face' and get to the core of things. Winning The Game Of Life is one such book. Kevin keeps things real, simple to grasp and easy to implement. Read it, feel it and dare yourself to really confront yourself, perhaps for the first time in your life to discover your True Self!

Mita Narottam, Image Consultant- www.mitanarottam.com

WINNING THE GAME OF LIFE has given me the confidence needed to be a successful business woman, I went through years of doubting my business plan only ever thinking of the what if's and the down falls I could face on my journey to entrepreneurship. 6months to date I finished THE GAME OF LIFE and it was the push I needed to start this business, In that short time I now have my CLOTHING LINE I've always wanted and STORE for retail ... "IF FAILURE WASNT AN OPTION THERE WOULD ONLY BE SUCCESS" THE GAME OF LIFE has changed my way of thinking and now looking to all positive outcomes.

BALLETTES- http://ballettes.blogtown.co.nz

I absolutely loved the book and what you are doing to inspire others to step out of the negative abyss. Awareness is often easier said than done, but you offer tools to keep people aware and motivated.

Mayra Veronica- International model

Step1: Remember your dreams.
Step2: Read Kevin's Book to help make them become an absolute reality.
Kevin's Book will give you the step by step tools to making your dreams
a reality.
Ish Jaddalah, Trader

"Excellent ideas and strategies for those seeking a greater life".
Tom Butler-Bowdon, author of 50 Success Classics,
50 Self-Help Classics www.Butler-Bowdon.com

"Remember the name Kevin Abdulrahman. Kevin is well on his way to inspire
millions of people with his "SECRET WEAPONS" I think anyone who truly
takes action on the principles Kevin lays out WILL be SUCCESSFUL!
Keep up the great work Kevin
Reed Floren, Internet marketer http://www.reedfloren.com/

The quality of your life will depend on what you feed your mind. In this
book, Kevin has created the breakfast for anyone wanting to excel and win.
Bob Urichuck, Author of Disciplined For Life:
You Are the Author of Your Future and Up Your Bottom Line;
Featuring the ABC, 123 Sales Results System.
Internationally Recognized Sales Guru -
Ranked # 7 in World's Top 30

THE BOOK
on
WINNING
the GAME
of LIFE

KEVIN ABDULRAHMAN

New York

THE BOOK on Winning The Game Of Life

Cover Design by: Rachel Lopez rachel@r2cdesign.com

ISBN 978-1-60037-614-6

Library of Congress Control Number: 2009925142

MORGAN · JAMES
THE ENTREPRENEURIAL PUBLISHER

Morgan James Publishing
1225 Franklin Ave., STE 325
Garden City, NY 11530-1693
Toll Free 800-485-4943
www.MorganJamesPublishing.com

In an effort to support local communities, raise awareness and funds, Morgan James Publishing donates one percent of all book sales for the life of each book to Habitat for Humanity. Get involved today, visit www.HelpHabitatForHumanity.org.

A gift from

_____

to you.

The Billionaires League Publishing
The Billionaires League Group of companies
Auckland, New Zealand
www.thisisTHEBOOK.com

Imagine gaining THE SECRET WEAPONS acquired by
those WINNING THE GAME of life. Enjoy the read and WIN YOUR GAME
in life, whatever it may be for you.

To the top

Kevin Abdulrahman

Who should read The Book?

The Book is for anyone who is serious about wanting to achieve great success in his or her life. Success is winning in anything that matters the most to you in your life. Life is a game, and unfortunately many are going through it without fully understanding how to play it.

Once you know how and what you need to play, you too can win the game of your life.

The Book is for anyone who wants to achieve the results that he or she isn't achieving.

It's for those who are achieving results but who feel that they can do more.

It's for those who want to know what sets the winners in life apart from the masses.
The Book is for those who want an edge.

The Book is for *you*.

To the memory of my loving dad, who passed away a lot earlier than his time, at the age of fifty-four. I hope I have made you proud, Dad. I have never stopped having you at my side. Your name is engraved on my heart. You were so rare.

And to my bright and alive mum, for her guidance. You shared with me THE SECRET WEAPONS that I am revealing in The Book, without my even realizing what you were sharing or understanding them completely at first …

… until I truly woke up.

I am only here today because of the two of you and the blessing of God.

You both are my ultimate blessing.

FOREWORD

One of my Boy Scouts has become a billionaire.

Another one of around the same time ended up in jail for attempted murder. Many have become successful business people; others have achieved less or more in other ways. From the same backgrounds, different people follow different paths and, of course, do not end up in the same place.

Why is this? Why are some people successful while others are seemingly not so successful? Much has been written over the last hundred years about success. Some say that we are born successful and that, for many, parents, society, schools, and universities take it away from us. Others suggest it is a choice we make.

Kevin Abdulrahman is one who has made a choice to be successful. "If success is the only option, then you are forced to succeed," he said. *The Book* chronicles what Kevin learned through his journey so far. It teaches the reader as he or she wishes it to. There is work to be done, or you can simply read through it. As in life, the reader has the choice of adopting or rejecting the wisdom contained within. From average beginnings, Kevin Abdulrahman has been able to move ahead in spite of such apparent limitations. He has said to the world, "Here I am, and I am on my way." Within twenty-seven short years, he has been able to do what most people struggle to do in a whole lifetime.

Between the covers of this book are endless pearls of wisdom. Some of these you will know already, and some will be completely new. That is the way of life. Kevin is the sum of thousands of years of human development. His wisdom has been passed to him from his parents and their parents before them. So it is with you. What Kevin has written here will add to your collective wisdom and speed you on to your personal path to success. You will of course choose how much of this collective wisdom from the book you add to your collection. I suggest you read it carefully.

Having known Kevin for some years now, I can attest to his extraordinary ability to learn and to teach. Still a young man, very young to some, he has much to offer this world. You may or may not agree with all he has to say.

I can assure you that it is all brought to you in a spirit of goodwill and that you may benefit from some or all of it.

There is much more to be said than is contained within *The Book on Winning the Game of Life*, so I would expect more to follow in either hard copy, digital, or recorded form.

Go well in your life. Continue to learn and gain personal mastery.

Yours,

David Payne

About Kevin Abdulrahman
'The Man Inspiring Millions'

Many of you may have already heard my story by now, but for those who haven't, here goes. Born in England to a Middle Eastern family, I am the eldest of three sons. Like many of you, growing up, I watched my parents bust their guts simply to make ends meet. They worked so hard, trying their very best and, as their kids, we got nothing close to the level of their efforts. We always lived in rented homes. Many weeks of every year, we would barely make it by. We did not live a poor life. It was average. We never went hungry, but we always worried about finances. Life revolved around how much money the family made and how much of it was washed away as overdrafts and bills.

The Gulf War caused a bit of unrest in our family, and after a period of searching around, we moved to New Zealand—a place I like to call paradise. Yet, even though we lived in paradise, nothing had changed. We had the same stress factors, the same situation, only now in a different place. We lived in paradise and, like many others, never stopped to enjoy the blessing we had living in such a beautiful place. We were in the so-called "field of roses," and yet, for the earlier years, we never had a chance to smell the roses. As a teenager, I was the kid who enjoyed his own company. Yeah, I would like to say I was a social butterfly but the reality was that I kept to myself. Going through school, I played cards with a few mates at lunch times and wasn't much of an athlete either. I came out of school and headed into university with all of two friends. I didn't have the greatest of foundations, and I certainly wasn't the most popular.

But let's go back a bit. Whilst at school, I worked hard at my part-time jobs. I did quite a few things, including paper runs, working in a supermarket, and a short, four-year stint working at McDonalds. I learned a lot from my part-time jobs. I took in a lot more than what I got paid from my weekly checks. I understood the meaning of commitment. When I signed up for the paper run, it was not a case of whether I was going to do it or not. I signed up for it, and now I had to do it—no ifs, buts, or maybes. The newspapers were expected to be in the designated letterboxes, rain, hail, or shine. From McDonalds, I learned the importance of systems and how an empire was built on something simple and easy to follow—a system that could be duplicated by anyone, anywhere. I also learned a lot about human interaction, and what made people do what they do. Every hour worked, although hard, was worth its weight in gold.

I learned a lot.

I was an average young guy with short, black hair and a goatee (an attempt to increase my cool factor). I was twenty years old, fresh out of university, and one word would have summed me up: frustrated.

I was frustrated because I didn't want to end up like my parents and most of the other people I saw around me. I mean no disrespect to my parents; they tried their very best. I knew that I could be successful if given the chance. I was lost. I was frustrated. I wanted to become successful, yet I didn't know how and no one around me did either. They all seemed to think they did, but I did not want the lives that they had. I was scared of failure. What would my friends say? I would prove those who said I was just another dreamer if I didn't make it. Not a chance—I would do whatever it took. I did not want to be poor anymore.

I was frustrated because, in my school holidays, I was working seventy to eighty-hour weeks. I chose to do them because I wanted to get ahead in life. I wanted to make more money. I thought working long hours was the answer. How naïve, how foolish. A few years on, I realized that hard work was not the answer. I also realized that my studies were only going to get me a job.

I wanted success. I wanted the lifestyle I had always dreamed of.

My first job offer straight after I finished my degree was to do voluntary work on a university project. I kindly declined their generous offer. I came to the simple realization that I was not happy with where I was in life. That hadn't changed during my university years. I was burdened with a loan, stacked high because of my tertiary education fees. I had nothing to my name except for a rusty vehicle worth four hundred dollars (if someone would even pay me for it). I knew I wanted to have a better life, and I knew that there were many places I wanted to go. I wanted to have the home I'd never had; I wanted the car of my dreams; I wanted to have the lifestyle. I knew what I wanted, and I wanted it badly.

I had a strong desire. The worst that could happen was that I would come back to where I was. I didn't want to be a passenger in life, living on other people's accord. I really had nothing to lose and everything to gain.

For your information, I excelled at making friends by now, and coming out of university, I had all of five friends.

From Flipping Burgers at Twenty to Being Retired at Twenty-five

In my journey to becoming a success, I learned a lot of lessons. I've taken lessons from everything and everyone I have ever had contact with. I've learned these lessons by seeing them in action and, on many occasions, wondering whether I could do the same. Everything I learned I put into practice. Every mistake I made only brought the desire to try again until I succeeded. Today, just a few short years on, my life is very different. I am living a life I could not have even imagined. How things have changed!

All because I made it my mission to have the life I want—to live life on my own terms, to do what I wanted to do, when I wanted to do it. I wanted to be able to spend my time with the people I cared about the most. It was a huge challenge but one worth striving for.

I conquered my quest of becoming a *success* in my own life. Today I am sharing what has helped me and many other successful people get to where we are.

Enjoy the read. I will see you at the top.

Kevin Abdulrahman 'The Man Inspiring Millions'

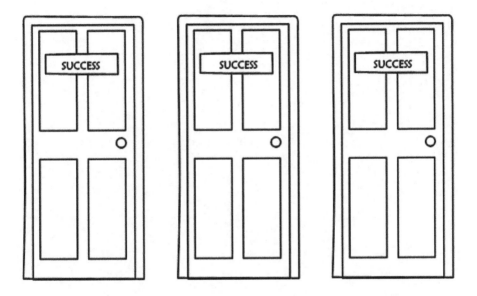

If success is the only option, then you are forced to succeed.
— Kevin Abdulrahman

PREFACE

I want to congratulate you for making a smart move in picking up this book. I commend you for your desire to excel in life. To become successful will require you to always be on a journey of discovery and learning. By the end of this book, you will know what has helped me achieve success and, in turn, have the opportunity to do the same in any aspect of your life. Success means different things to different people, but the principles behind achieving it are the same. Life is a game, and to achieve success is equivalent to winning the game that you are playing. Since success will have different meanings for each reader, I shall be referring to it as winning the game of life. To achieve whatever you need to achieve, you need to win the game you are playing. When you do so, you achieve your great success.

It seems like most people want to achieve great success in life but lack the knowledge of going about it in the right way. Everyone wants success in some shape and form, yet many fail to attain it. Many think that the hurdles that they face are equivalent to that of a concrete block. What if I told you that the hurdles are nothing but a small bubble? Most people are seemingly stuck in a small bubble trying to burst through but to no avail. Acquiring the secret weapons that I share in The Book will not only help you burst through the bubble but propel you towards your destination much faster.

But do you have what it takes to win the game?

Do you have the potential to become a success in your own right?

If someone else has done it, is that not enough proof that you can do it too?

The simple answer is yes.

So the million-dollar question lingers: Why did I write this book?

The second question is why am I even sharing it with you?

Both are fair questions.

I am not a professional writer. What I'm sharing with you comes straight from the heart. I was recommended to get a ghostwriter and have things made perfect but thought that it would take away from the essence of what I was sharing. This book is designed to be my way of communicating with you, as if we're catching up over a latte, discussing what is required for you to win the game of your life. What you will read are my thoughts that I've put on paper as I've gone through the journey and won the game in my life.

I wrote this book in order to make a difference in the lives of people who are working hard and giving their very best (just like my parents, my friends, and most other people) yet come home at the end of the day dissatisfied and unfulfilled because they are getting far too little output, relative to what they are putting in. I have seen many people try to model other successful people in what they do yet be unable to achieve the results they had hoped for.

What I share in The Book are the secret weapons that successful people possess. It is these weapons that set them apart.

The weapons possessed by successful people are, in many instances, not known to them. Some of these successful people acquired them and are consciously aware of having done so, but for most, the ability to use these weapons is an innate characteristic. No wonder the masses can't mirror or model those who are successful. If successful people are unaware of their own secret weapons, then how can someone who wants the same results possibly achieve them? Successful people have, at some point, acquired them and practiced them and are true masters in utilizing these weapons. Once you know about these weapons, you will need to put them into practice and become a master of utilizing them in order to be able to win your game of life.

How many people do you know who feel the frustration of not winning their game? How many people do you know who lie awake at night just wondering how on earth will things ever change? Just like most people today, I was extremely frustrated with life and wanted so much more. I knew that life had much more to offer, and I certainly didn't seem to be getting my fair share of it. I wanted to live life on my terms. I wanted what everyone wants—success.

In the quest for winning the game of life, I watched and studied successful people in different fields. I looked at what made them stand out from the masses. I started to notice what they were involved in and, most importantly, how they went about doing things. It was much harder than I initially anticipated. Like many, I figured that if I simply copied what a successful person does, then I could have what they had. That held a certain amount of truth, but it was not the answer. I noticed that for every successful person, there were thousands of others doing the same things and yet not getting the same results. This seemed to be the case in just about every single aspect of life. I saw it in friendships, relationships, sports, work environments and business. I began to question these occurrences. Why was such a thing happening? Where were the gaps? What were the missing links? Why were the results still so different? What was missing by most that was held by those who were successful? It just seemed unfair that most people tried and yet failed. So what secret weapons did successful people possess?

Those were the questions. The Book will provide you with the answers.

I have dedicated my work to making a difference in people's lives.

My intention is simple. It is to get every person on this planet to learn about these weapons and utilize them in their own lives to make a change for the better. If you walk away with just a few points that can help you obtain the lifestyle you deserve, then I will consider my book to be a success. Help me to spread this message by sharing your recommendation of The Book (www. thisisTHEBOOK.com) with at least three friends. They will always have you to thank for giving them the heads up.

So what do I get out of it? My motivation (and my reward) are both selfish and selfless. My selfish reward is a sense of achievement. My selfless reward is a sense of happiness, knowing that I could make a difference in the lives of millions—that one day people will remember me as the man who inspired millions, the man who instilled the seeds of success in them. That is the ultimate happiness.

I have designed this book to be easy to read. It is in plain English and is divided into clearly defined chapters. My intention for this book is that it can be read and appreciated by a person from any walk of life or age group. I want you to be able to pick it up and read any one of the chapters to get one new tip to implement in your life. This organization will also make it easy for you to come back and refresh your memory down the track on any particular points you may want to run your eyes over.

I used to play video games in my younger days and loved every moment of it. I realized that, if I applied the same principles that helped me win in video games to my life, then I could win the game of life. It worked. I hope it will sit well with where you are today or at least spark a memory and take you back to when you held a controller and stared at the TV playing video games. This analogy helped me achieve immense success in life. It was my perspective and it served me well. Combined with learning from my teachers, this way of thinking was the perfect match. Just like in a game, I had infinite chances to get it right in life, so long as I was willing to play. As a result, I was able to "find my treasure chest," metaphorically speaking.

At times in a game, some places are dark, and a torch would be a useful weapon. At times, we are battling through a rough patch, and we could do with strong armor. Other times, we are forced to attack so as not to lose the ground we have covered.

Think of some of your favorite video games (Street Fighter, Pac-Man, Sonic the Hedgehog, Crash Bandicoot, World of Warcraft, Command & Conquer, or Counter-Strike). Think of the game you played the most. The time spent playing that game could very much be the key to unlocking your potential to achieve success in your life. As I take you through each chapter, think back to a scene of yourself playing the game of your choice. See if you can relate back to it and then match it with real life. That way you will always be able to recall the weapon when you need to use it.

At the end of each chapter, I have included space for you to make notes, as well as exercises that you must complete. The purpose of this is to take your learning to the next level by having you play an active part in the process. Ensure that you do these exercises as you go, as this will help you truly grasp the essence of each weapon. You will be asked to describe what you observe about yourself in relation to each weapon and how you can implement that weapon into your own life. Based on what you have read in each chapter you will recognize whether you are on the right path or whether change is required.

So grab a pen now.

I ask you to keep an open mind when reading through The Book. I hope that you will relate to most of what I say. It is real and from the heart. You may feel that some of the weapons I describe go against some of the things that you have known. Aim not to fight what you are learning; rather, evaluate with an open mind whether the concept could make a difference in bettering your life.

Be certain to read and reread this book a second or third time. Every time you pick this book up, you will be in a different headspace and will be receptive to different aspects. It is guaranteed that different things will jump out at you and have a stronger impression on you the second and third time around.

Through reading this book, you will discover THE SECRET WEAPONS that will enrich your day-to-day activities and get you to where you would like to be in life. I ask you to take each weapon on board and put them into action.

ACKNOWLEDGMENTS

This book would not have happened had it not been for a series of events that led me to this point in my life. I am eternally grateful for every single moment—the good and the not so good.

The environment I was subjected to and the experiences I had greatly influenced my decision—the decision to break through what seemed to be the fate of a mediocre life. My parents worked so hard to raise my younger brothers and me to understand that we could have everything we wanted in life. Their efforts were the foundation of my success. I also learned the mentality of never cutting myself short of anything I wanted. This little grain was instilled early in my life. I aim to instill that in you throughout The Book, so that you too can be the best that you can be.

I would like to thank all of my direct and indirect teachers who I have had so far. Many have been my teachers without knowing so. I've had teachers who have guided not only the things I wanted to be and have, but who have shown me the things I didn't want to be or have in my own life.

Thank you to everyone who has been close to me. You

know who you are; you are my family. I want to thank the true friends who have stuck by my side throughout the ups and many downs. I also want to thank those who laughed at me (or behind my back) throughout my journey and those who ended up not being the truest of friends. You were all a strong reason for my success. You have all impacted my life in such a positive way, and I learned a lot about human nature in the process. Thank you.

I want to thank my two younger brothers, who have always believed in their "crazy brother" when my dreams seemed rather farfetched to them and who are also always quick to keep me grounded when the need arises. I want to thank the lady in my life, who had to endure me through out the many challenges we have faced- I can't ever thank you enough.

My sincere thanks to the team at Morgan James Publishing and immense gratitude to my initial proof reader Robyn Irons. I want to thank everyone who has helped me—with his or her skills and knowledge, honest opinions, and sense of support to get The Book to print. To name all the people who have helped me out in one way or another would require a book of its own. You all know who you are, and I am ever grateful to you.

Lastly I want to thank you, the reader, in advance for, hopefully, allowing the content of this book to get to your heart, mind, and soul. I look forward to hearing about your success.

Here's to you winning the game of life

WARNING

The Book on Winning the Game of Life is simple and straightforward. It will offend some, but the content will always be truthful. It will only be useful to those who will seriously do something with THE SECRET WEAPONS they obtain.

The Book will give to you as much as you put in to it.

You have been warned ...

CONTENT

"Know where to find the information and how to use it. That's the secret to success"

— Albert Einstein, Nobel Prize winning physicist

01

*"I've got all the money I'll ever need,
if I die by four o'clock"*

– Henny Youngman (Comedian)

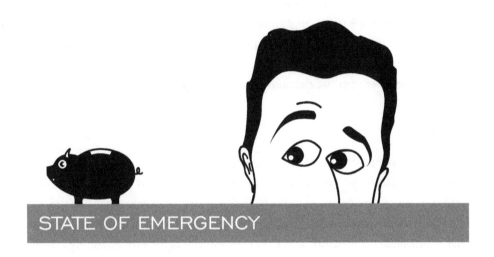

STATE OF EMERGENCY

WE ARE IN A STATE OF EMERGENCY

How many people do you know who complain, "I'm too healthy," "I have too much time," or "I have too much money"?

When was the last time you heard someone complain like that?

Houses prices have nearly doubled in the last decade. How many incomes have you seen double? In the last few years, people have watched property prices rocket through the roof. Most people's income has not kept up, and hence, more and more people are, unfortunately, losing the simple dream of owning their own home.

Gas prices are pretty high (not at the premium of what bottled water is selling for, but nonetheless) and is set only to go up. The cost of food and other expenses is on the increase, so why is it that most people are still working in what seems like a flawed model, achieving a mediocre life?

It used to be that one family member, mum or dad, would support the household. Today, both parents have to go to work to keep the same standard of living of only a few short years ago. As a result, people are spending less time with the people they care about most. Parents are working so hard, trying their very best, and yet their families are in desperate need of them. They are in desperate need of family time. Sure their family members appreciate the money, and they appreciate the roof over their heads and the food on the table, but the reality is their loved ones need their time. Time is the single most important thing you can ever give. Yet so many parents today are not able to fulfill this important need, not because they don't want to but, in fact, because of desperation, and it's not looking to get any better. The gap between the rich and poor is increasing at an *alarming rate*.

Why?

Why are people shortchanging themselves? Some do it voluntarily. Others just don't know how to get out of the rut or, in some cases, that doing so is even an option. Some people may seem like they are winning the *donkey race*, but they are still living the sad lives of donkeys. How come only a select few live the lifestyles they want? Here is the reality, and I am sure you will agree with me on this. Some people have no money and a lot of time, while others have no time and some money, but *most* people have no money and no time. That's true for the majority of people all over the world.

Hence I will reiterate that we have a worldwide *state of emergency*.

GAME TIME

Imagine you are playing a video game and, from the beginning, you don't seem to know how to move ahead. You just can't seem to find the path you must take. It's a blur. You are trying to go all around the screen, left, right, sideways, but because you don't know the correct path, you can't seem to move ahead. You keeping moving in circles, but nothing happens. Your frustration is at the highest level because you don't know what you are supposed to do. At this point, those who lack the patience usually give up and stop playing the game—unless, of course, someone who has successfully played the game before shares with them how to make the secret door appear. He or she may have the cheat sheet of simple ways to play the game a lot more smoothly. This person mentions to you that it would be a combination of just a few simple moves and, voilà, the door appears. You listen to every word this person says because he or she has played it to the end. He or she has *clocked* it. You take on the tips, put them into practice, and enjoy winning the game.

You have now started your game to achieve your ultimate life so that you can become a success in whatever you wish to do and be—having the *money* and the *time* to do what you please whenever you wish to do so and with whomever you wish to be with. You may want to apply what you learn in your friendships, relationships, sports, job, or business.

Can this be learned at school?
I will let Mark Twain answer that:

"I have never let my schooling interfere with my education."
—Mark Twain, the father of American literature

Why is success not taught at school? Why is it not taught at universities? Why is it that many people are taught to use a flawed model and to do things that are obviously not getting the results they want? I have personally learned a lot by going to school and obtaining a university degree. I do advise everyone to get some sort of education.

But herein lies the issue: Unfortunately, to teach success one must be successful in at least one aspect of life. Many schools don't have successful people spending their time teaching others. Today, people are realizing that they need to be in control of their lives if they want to get ahead in any aspect. It's not only the younger generation that is facing this crisis; there are fifty- and sixty-year-olds who today still don't know THE SECRET WEAPONS to winning the game of life.

The rich seem to get richer. The poor seem to get poorer. And it seems like the middle class pays for both. The middle class, to me, is being mediocre. Life seems good, but they are paying a big price for being there. Being mediocre is the worst thing to choose because being mediocre is neither here nor there. Being mediocre limits the potential of becoming great; in fact, it is the biggest enemy of greatness. Being mediocre is for those who don't want a full life. The first SECRET WEAPON successful people acquire and master is *choosing to excel*—in any aspect of life that is important to them. You, and only you, can choose where you would like to be in life, at the top of your game, or at the bottom of it. Successful people have mastered the weapon at always *choosing to excel* in whatever they do. It could be the first day on the job, a new field, a new challenge, a new sport, a new business or friendships and other personal relationships. Successful people go through the learning phase with the end in mind. The end they have in mind is to become *great* at whatever it is that they have chosen to do because they have realized that nobody remembers second best.

You are in the game, and you are going through challenges as they come by. Can the person who has never played this game be of any help to you? Can people tell you where to jump and duck if they haven't played or ever progressed to the level you want to get to? So how can you *choose to excel?*

Life is what you make of it. The trick is to make the most of it by knowing how to use the resources available to you. Educate yourself at school, but never settle for mediocre. Settling is the biggest injustice you will do to yourself and to the people you care about most. Aim to constantly *excel* in life. Increase your learning by reading more books, listening to more CDs, and attending seminars about whatever interests you. More people are waking up to the fact that you must *self-educate*. Your education is your responsibility and no one else's. Seek the answers you desire and become the best in whatever you choose to do.

Here's a vision I am putting out there:

I would love to see schools have a SUCCESS DAY. Maybe once every few months, schools should arrange for successful people in their local area to talk to a class on success in their field, to inspire today's youth. I envision speakers from different age groups and walks of life sharing their thoughts in practical, simple English with students who are still studying at school. I truly believe that if we could harness the mind of the youth and teach success at an early age, millions of people would benefit from seemingly small inspirations and mind shifts. It is amazing what could be done simply by instilling some seeds of greatness into the youth of today. They will shape the future.

It's never too late to learn. It does not matter if you are twelve or eighty; now is better than never. I always say that if you gain at least one point out of any meeting, class, lecture, presentation, CD, or book, then you have moved one step ahead, and your investment has more than paid off. Like everything in life, what you learn comes down to you. If you go in wanting to learn, you will always benefit from any situation. Go in to learn. Your learning power will equate to your earning power.

Teachers have an important role in our society. They are, however, overworked and underpaid. In terms of financial or life success, a small percentage of teachers are classified as successful. By no means am I devaluing or disrespecting this valuable profession. However, I do see the need to have people who have walked the walk help in integrating some learning with real life experiences.

"The spirit, the will to win, and the will to excel are the things that endure. These qualities are so much more important than the events that occur."
—Vince Lombardi, American football coach

Think of the highest paid individuals. They have chosen to excel in their fields. They stand out and will always charge a premium, but people will happily pay. They have earned it.

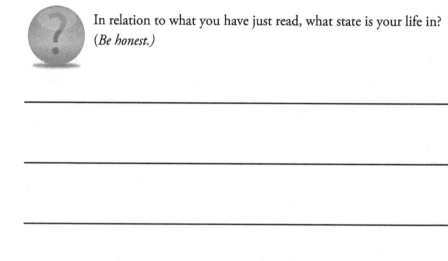

In relation to what you have just read, what state is your life in? (*Be honest.*)

_____

_____

_____

What two things *must* you do to excel toward winning your game of life?

_____

_____

_____

Take Home Message

In this day and age when we are in a state of emergency, the worst thing we could do with our lives is to be mediocre. Choose to excel and become great.

02

"*When the going gets tough,
the tough fight back*"

— Kevin Abdulrahman

LETTING IT HAPPEN
VS MAKING IT HAPPEN

Here is a challenge for you:

See if you relate to any of the following statements.

I want you to be honest with yourself. Each answer is a simple *yes* or *no* that you can tick off.

You are content with your life but realize that you have the potential to achieve more.

Yes ☐   No ☐

You work hard, but you are *not* living the ideal life you always envisaged.

Yes ☐   No ☐

You work hard, and yet, your family is *not* getting the best of you.

Yes ☐   No ☐

You spend many days of the week frustrated with yourself.

Yes ☐   No ☐

Bluntly speaking, there could be more to your life than the one you are currently living.

Yes ☐   No ☐

You have realized it is time to play a smarter game.

Yes ☐   No ☐

You understand that it is insane to keep on doing the same things and expect a different result.

Yes ☐   No ☐

You are willing to do whatever it takes to win the game of your life.

Yes ☐   No ☐

If your answer is yes to most of my statements, I want to tell you that you are not alone. Many people feel this way. A few short years ago, I answered *yes* to all of the above. I used to feel frustrated every day. I was giving it my best, but the results were not showing. I was in a state of emergency as I explained earlier. Enough was enough. Something had to change!

Would you like to turn your life from a state of emergency to a state of euphoria and success? A state of happiness and fulfillment?

Then it's time to make a smart move.

It is time for you to *take control*!!

The second SECRET WEAPON that successful people in all fields acquire is *taking control* of their lives—not just during the good times; they take control all the time. If something good happens in their life, they know it is because of their direct efforts and actions. In contrast, if things don't go as planned, they know that the finger points only at them. Mastering this weapon means that there is no pointing the finger at anyone but the person in control. And that person is you. Most people are quick to mention their contribution should something go according to plan, yet they are the first to point fingers when things go wrong. You will notice that these people are far from successful. Successful people take ownership of the decisions they make, the good and the bad.

Remember that no one will ever want success more for you than you. To think otherwise is delusional. I see people living life thinking their family, friends, or strangers will someday give them what they want in life. You have a better chance of winning the lottery.

You are the only person who can control things in your life. If things are not going according to plan, then something needs to change. For things to change, you must change. For your results to change, you must change what you are doing. Ultimately, though, making a change is in your control.

Will it come at a price? *Absolutely.*

But that is not the question. The question is, what price are you currently paying by not taking control? Compare this with the price you must pay to take control and have the life of your dreams.

Either way, you will pay the price. Thus, choose to pay the right price and live the life you deserve. *Take control.*

GAME TIME

Remember who holds the controller when you are playing a game. You are in complete control of your life. Sure, there are challenges flying your way, but only you are in control of your maneuvering. You can go back, forward, up, down, or sideways. You can jump, stand still, or roll over. If you don't like where you are in the game, then you move forward. If you stand still whilst in combat mode, you will be killed. You are in charge of defending yourself and moving ahead in the game. The end will not come to you. You must get to the end. You will get scared, you will get hit, and you will get defeated on occasion, but you will survive and move forward. You are the person in control.

"If you can't, you must. If you must, you can."
—Anthony Robbins, a top authority on peak performance

When it comes to taking control, successful people do not try. They make *taking control a* must. Think of a time when something in your life became a must. You just had to do it. There were no ifs, buts, or maybes.

When you absolutely have to do something, you just do it. Try never comes into the equation

"I'm trying, Kevin, but I just can't get my business off the ground." or "Kevin, I am trying to compete in the Olympics, but I can't seem to qualify."

Every time I hear the word "try," the term *"definite maybe"* comes to my mind. When you say the word "try," you are already implying you will *not* do it.

I want you to try and write your full name here so that if you misplace *The Book*, someone may be kind enough to see this and mail it back to you.

Name: _____

Address: _____

Best contact number: _____

Did you do it? Did you fill in your details?

You either wrote your name, or you didn't. There were no ifs, buts, or maybes.

Humor me for a second. Ever tried to go to the bathroom when nature calls? I'm talking about when it really calls? Or did you somehow make it happen? You get there one way or another because it is a must for you. It just happens. You do your business.

Think of women in general for a second. All of us have or have had mums at some point and time. Did they try to bring us into this world? No, they just did it.

If someone you care about is in danger, do you try to help them, or do you just get on and *do it?*

Either you *do* or you *don't*. It's that simple.

"Just Do It."
—Nike

What I am getting at is that the word "try" shouldn't even exist. In fact, if I had it my way, I would make the use of the word "try" illegal. Ban it from your vocabulary. Make everything that is important in your life a must.

Taking control applies to every aspect of your life. Here are a few situations where many don't practice taking control. See if any apply to you.

You wake up in the morning and, just as you decide to have a good day, you check the mailbox. *Whaaam!* There are five bills to pay, two of which are unexpected and rather large. You spend the rest of the day depressed.

You have a business appointment with a client who has agreed to make a purchase. An hour before your meeting, you get a call from your client informing you that he or she no longer will proceed with the purchase. You spend the rest of the day resentful.

You are on your way home, and the person in front of you cuts you off. You get angry and let out a few words that come from the school of frustration. You spend the rest of the day fuming.

There are two types of people in this world—those who are controlled by their environment and those who control their environment. In the second group are the successful people. Successful people know how to take control of their environment, never letting others dictate what they do or, more importantly, how they feel.

Which of the two types are you?

Does your environment control you? Or do you control your environment?

Could you choose not to let things affect you? Most people live life in reaction to the events and circumstances that surround them. People let their environment or circumstances dictate what they do, when and where they do what they do, and how they think, feel, and act. Why?

Rather than reacting, look at living a life based on your desires and requirements. Act based upon the focus of what you want in order to achieve it. People who are distracted by everything happening in their surroundings do not excel because they are so caught up with insignificant events. Many people behave in a reactive way to changes that occur in their life. They spend countless hours, days, weeks, even years dwelling on past events. Their time and energy is spent. When people are driving on the highway, it is as if most of them spend more time focusing on the bugs hitting their windshield than the road they are traveling on.

Incidents happen all the time. Think of them as the bugs that hit your windshield. The key is to simply take control of the wheel and look beyond the bugs to the road ahead, as you focus on getting to your destination. That doesn't mean that you deny the fact that things can happen, and oh yes, things will happen. Work on being in complete control as you come across challenging circumstances in life. It may be daunting at first, just like taking your first baby steps, but have you thought about walking lately? Very quickly, new skills become natural.

Are you just going to linger long enough, in the hope that something miraculous will happen in your life? Or will you actively do something about your life?

In American football, you can play the game on the offense or on the defense. The game of life must be played one way and one way only—on the offense. You must always be one step ahead of the game if you want to win. If you are going to play on the defense, you will end up watching things happen. Successful people always make their moves and preempt the surrounding moves of other people and of circumstances. Playing defense will never get you the results you want. Play the game on the offense and account for your surrounding moves in advance. Again, this will come with practice. The more you do this, the easier it will become. If you truly learn to take control, you will be the first to forgive in a situation. You will be the first to admit your mistakes. You will be the first to make a move on a sale or sign a business deal. You will be the first to show kindness. You will create the energy and motion for others to follow.

Wouldn't the world be a better place when more people start to *take control*?

GAME TIME

When you are playing the game, do you ponder for hours on end why you died or fell in the hole? No. You simply wait until you reappear on the screen (usually in a few seconds) and get on with it. Do the same in your life.

How have you been living your life? Are you taking control? (*Be honest.*)

What two things *must* you do to help you take control in winning your game of life?

Take Home Message

Take control. Don't let things happen; learn to make them happen.

03

"He who fails to plan, plans to fail"

— Ancient proverb

YOU ARE PLANNING TO FAIL!

Where are you now? Where is your life today? How does it rate on a scale of 1 – 10—1 being miserable and 10 being *euphoric?*

1   2   3   4   5   6   7   8   9   10

If you were to go back five short years and think of what you had envisaged your life to be today, would you say you have everything you wanted? (Be honest.)

Yes ☐   No ☐

If your life was a destination, have you arrived today? Or are you still miles away from your destination?

Have you today achieved everything that you wanted to five years ago? Did you even think about setting a target for today? If you haven't, ask yourself this: How could you shoot a bull's-eye if the target doesn't exist?

Most people, after spending a bit of time reflecting and being honest with themselves, come to an unfortunate and rather shocking truth. Most have hoped to be in a better place compared to where they are today. By not setting themselves up with a target, they have planned to fail.

It may sound ridiculous, but most people are inadvertently planning to fail. Why do I say that? I mean, you don't hear people coming up to you and saying, "Oh by the way, I have just finished planning how I can fail this year and do a good job at it." You would never hear someone actually say that, yet nine times out of ten, we know of people who have ended up getting that *failed* result. Why is that?

Although many never plan to fail, they fail to plan the route ahead. They fail to plan their road map, their strategy in order to *win the game*. Most people spend more time doing their hair in the morning or planning their summer holidays than thinking about what they truly want out of life. By failing to plan they have, with complete intention, *planned to fail*. Could this be true of someone you know? Could this be you?

I am not only talking about planning for the big things. Planning is important for all aspects of your life—from the big goals to the smaller, day-to-day occurrences. One day, I was driving back from Wellington, New Zealand's capital, to Auckland, the city of sails. I was three-quarters of the way there when I noticed my fuel gauge indicating that I was running on the reserve fuel. Upon arriving in the next town, I had a delicious Thai dinner and relaxed for a short while before the last stretch of the journey. I did not, however, make any plans or decisions to fill up my fuel tank. I hit the road, and let me tell you, the next forty kilometers were filled with a lot of stress. It was dark by now, and I was driving along side roads. There wasn't a car in sight going either way, and I could feel the car losing power due to the lack of fuel. I kept on driving, praying the whole way. I could not believe that I'd noticed but hadn't made any plan to stop at a petrol station. I felt so stupid. It truly got me thinking about life and how we literally see things but do not make a clear intention of planning to do things. Did I plan to have a stressful forty-kilometer drive? Ultimately, I did. It's harsh, but it's true.

"It pays to plan ahead. It wasn't raining when Noah built the ark."
—Thomas Edison, most famous American inventor

When things are planned, they tend to happen. When things are planned, there is a clear intention to execute the plan. There is no room to forget when you seriously plan for something. This would apply to relationships too. How many times have you missed a special day of a loved one? The chances are, you did not plan to have that day scheduled out or did not plan to get a gift.

One Christmas I forgot to get my girlfriend a gift. She couldn't believe it. I couldn't believe it. We both sat there in shock. I couldn't believe that it had slipped my mind, considering we did the Christmas shopping together. I did not plan for the time needed to get her a gift and, quite simply, got caught up with everything and ended up empty-handed. Let's just say that, to this day, I get reminded of my *stupidity* on every special occasion.

I can tell you that the key to my success in achieving a healthier and fitter body than I used to have has come from planning and training with my personal trainer. I made a plan with him and worked on executing it every day. It was so simple and yet so effective; bit by bit, that training gave me immense changes over six weeks. Up until then, I always talked about losing weight and putting on some muscle mass. My friends know that I talked about it for two years, but nothing was changing. I knew I had what it takes to have a good physique, but I didn't plan to have one. So every time I halfheartedly tried to start losing weight, sure as the sun rising from the east, I was not getting the results I wanted. Then my friends noticed changes and commented on them. They asked me what I did. I simply replied, "I planned. I executed. I conquered."

Remember, there are no second chances in life because time is very unforgiving. We only get one shot at living every day, so you might as well make it your best. We only get second chances in getting it right. Here is your chance now.

Let's fast forward five short years into the future. Would you like things to be different?

Yes ☐   No ☐

Doing what you've done in the last five years has gotten you to this particular place in life today. If this place is far from what you had hoped, then I think it's fair to say that you should ask yourself, "Doing what I'm doing today, will I achieve everything I want in the next five years?"

GAME TIME

There are two types of people who play the game—those who are serious about conquering the levels and those who are just playing around. Now if you are playing around, that's fine because not every person takes video games so seriously. But if you are serious, it's time to step it up. What has passed has passed, but you are being given a second chance if you have wasted your first. In this game, you have unlimited lives, so as long as you are a willing contender, the game is on. It's time to get going. It's time to step up your game. You're getting to a level where you'll be learning about acquiring weapons that will help you move forward in leaps and bounds. You are where you are in your game because of the moves you have made; to move ahead smarter, you will have to learn and apply smarter weapons. You use the map on the left of your screen to see where you are and where you want to go well in advance of arriving there. Doing so will help you play smarter. You will get to the checkpoints a lot quicker, and you will become stronger and stronger as you move ahead.

Grab a pen and take the time to complete the exercise either in the space provided or on a clean sheet of paper, which you can refer to every day. I suggest that you participate fully so you can get the most out of this book.

I want you to consider this. It is five years from now. You wake up in the morning, and today is the start of your dream life. Neither money nor time are an object; you can do whatever you want, wherever you want, and with whomever you want to do it. Write down exactly all the things you want in your life in the next five years on the above terms. This is a movie script of your dream life. Everything you include you will have, and everything you miss out will not be provided, so be greedy for once and have everything that you desire. Don't leave anything out. Remember, if you could live your life any way you want, here is your chance. Go ahead; write out a movie script of *your dream life*.

Here are some prompts to get you thinking.

Have a housekeeper	Travel through New Zealand
Get on the Oprah show	Take a bunch of friends on vacation
Build an orphanage	Safari in Africa
Go and see extended family	Request a bowl of blue peanut M&M's
Spoil yourself	Sleep in until you wake up
Spoil the people you love	Have a super yacht
Own seven super cars	Pull off a convincing April Fool's trick
Own a private jet	See the Seven Wonders of the World (old and new)
Get a college education	Donate to charity in a significant way
Enroll kids in private schools	Travel first class
Build a hospital	Stay at the finest hotels and resorts
Travel with loved ones	Follow the Grand Prix Circuit
Enjoy fine dining	Go surfing
Take dancing lessons	Follow the Tour de France
Start the day with a full body massage	Become a millionaire
Shop till you drop	Retire early
Send a message in a bottle	Do some public speaking

Swim with dolphins   Do a bungee jump

Stand on the equator   Work for charity

Go to every single theme park there is   Live in the tallest tower in Dubai

---

Now for some *serious* questions that you must ask yourself.

Doing what I am doing *right now*, am I going to achieve my dream life?

Yes ☐   No ☐   On the fence ☐

If you are on the fence, the answer is *no.*

If what you are doing is not getting you there, then you must ask yourself this:

Do I have a second shot at living today?

Yes ☐   No ☐

Will things change if I keep on doing what I am doing?

Yes ☐   No ☐

Am I expecting things to change without me changing?

Yes ☐   No ☐

If yes, check for *sanity.*

Am I willing to work hard and smart to get what I want?

Yes ☐   No ☐

So you read the shocking truth earlier: Most people are *planning to fail.*

The third SECRET WEAPON that successful people develop is *planning and executing.* They usually do this behind the scenes, but it *gets done.* This is another weapon that the majority of people don't see. Successful people find out exactly where they are and where they want to go. They plan, and they execute. They have a thirty-day, a ninety-day, a one-year, a three-year, a five-year, a ten-year, and a hundred-year plan. When you hear a success story in any field, very rarely do you hear the term *plan* alongside the story. Most people don't see the background work that was required for the successful person to attain that level of success, yet it is a crucial weapon used by everyone who has achieved success in any field.

"Those who plan do better than those who do not plan, even though they rarely stick to their plan."
—Winston Churchill, former British prime minister

Take some time to plan for every aspect in life that is important to you. Plan for the dream life you have just written about. A plan is never set in concrete but provides you with guidelines to help you achieve everything you desire. You can change your plan along the way, and in many cases, your plan will change as you progress.

Have you planned and executed effectively so far in your life? (*Be honest.*)

Reading this book will help you recognize and apply THE SECRET WEAPONS you'll need to get you from where you are now to where you want to be.

Are you going to be dedicated and serious in applying THE SECRET WEAPONS?

Yes ☐   No ☐

Based on what you have read, have you ever planned to fail? If so, how? (*Be honest.*)

_____

_____

What are the two things you must to do *right now* in order to achieve the life you desire?

_____

_____

 Take Home Message

The next five years will only be different from the last five years if you plan them.

Plan, execute, and conquer.

"*All that we are is the result of what we have thought*"

– Buddha

EVERYTHING IN LIFE IS A RESULT

I am working as hard as I can. I have been making twenty calls a day. I have been working out for the last three years. I buy flowers for my partner every month, but our relationship is far from passionate. I have done four hundred presentations for my business and have not had a single sale yet. I can't seem to cross to the next level in my sport.

Does any of this sound familiar?

Hard work, energy, blood, sweat, and tears—to deduce a few of the payments people make in the pursuit of success from the above list of complaints—don't mean anything. It's also unfortunate that the majority of people only focus on what they do rather than the results they're getting. The results of what you put in are what comprise your score card. What is on the score card is all that matters. Results are all that matters. You have either seen or experienced what would be classified as unfair situations, such as the following examples:

• A person working and trying hard to achieve a certain sales target, while another colleague cruises by with, seemingly, a lot less effort

• Two people going to the gym—as an outsider, you would say that person A is working really hard in the gym compared to person B; yet person B has the better results in twelve weeks

• Two students studying for their exams, one studying a lot more than the other; yet the one who seemingly studied less gets the better grades

It seems unfair. I used to say that. But that is the reality. What makes these so-called *underdogs* win?

They do the right things needed to get the results. They do the smart things that matter. Everything in life has a formula. Get the formula right, and you get the right result. The results you have in your life right now will tell you something about what you are putting into it. Successful people have an orientation for the outcome. They have mastered the fourth SECRET WEAPON—being *results orientated.* Everything is based on results—not the resources spent on something, not the time taken, not how much energy was put into something, none of that. It is simply all about the *results.* This is another secret weapon successful people possess in their arsenal that helps them move ahead in leaps and bounds.

Wherever you are in your life is a result, whether you like it or not. Your weight is a result. Your health is a result. Your relationship status is a result. Your cash flow is a result, and your net worth is a result.

Results, results, results—results are all that matter.

If any of the results in your life need changing, then you must review what you are doing. As the famous saying goes, if you keep on doing what you have always done, then you will keep on getting what you have always gotten.

"Successful people give you results. Others will give you their rationale."
—Kevin Abdulrahman

To change your financial results, you must change what you are doing or how you are doing it. And you must do so *now*. To change your sporting result, you need to change what you do or how you are doing it, And *now*.

You are not getting the result you desire, and you have tried and tried and tried. There is no point banging your head against a brick wall wanting to get to the other side. Don't try to rationalize why you are not getting the results. It's a waste of energy. Instead try another avenue; maybe there's a different path that another person who is achieving the result you want is using, and maybe you could do the same. Chances are, if her or she is achieving the desired result, so can you.

Do you want to be mediocre or successful?

Do you want to be forgotten or remembered?

Do you want to live a full life or one where you constantly ask yourself, "Could I have done that?"

A very successful person always told me to be a "results-based person." Since then, I have taken on being *results orientated*. Today, talk is cheap to me. Anyone can talk, and a lot of people do a lot of talking. I have found that only a few people will materialize what they talk about and, hence, I deal only with those people in my day-to-day activities. I am more interested in results than talk.

Results are also what I coach people on!

You must develop and master this weapon of being *results orientated*. Your result could mean achieving a specific ranking in your business organization. It could mean attaining certain financial success or hitting certain targets at work. Or your result could be winning the *gold* at the next Olympics. Getting results, for you, could be having the ability to choose how to spend your days without any worries, the ability to go to the beach and sip from a coconut knowing your finances are of no concern. Your result could be the ability to give the best to your family—your *time*. It could be spending two full days of every week with the people you love and care about the most; it could be the time you spend giving to others.

To help you master the weapon of being *results orientated,* I will share with you the concept of living life by design, as opposed to living life by default. As I touched on in the previous chapter, the masses are living every day of their lives by default, with no plan whatsoever, hoping that things will stack up in their favor. Unfortunately, the majority of people think this way, and hence, their end results are not what they'd wished for.

When you live life by design (in other words, when you plan), you have the results in mind and can move ahead, constantly tweaking every step on the way if need be. For example, when I was working at McDonalds, we (the kitchen crew) had to be able to make twelve cheeseburgers in less than ninety seconds. The twelve cheeseburgers were the *results* we had to achieve within a time frame. Everything else was simply a process to get there. Imagine if we had no idea of what result was expected for that ninety seconds; we would be standing there scratching our heads wondering what we were doing. The store would have crumbled over night—a disaster, to say the least.

When you live life by design, you are the one calling the shots and, believe it or not, you will start getting the results you want. You plan and then take action steps to achieve the result within a certain time frame. Here are three quick tips to steer you on the right track to achieve *results.*

1. Do what other successful people in your area of interest are doing. In other words, you cannot spend your time in cooking classes if you want to be a top badminton player. You must learn and play with the best on the badminton court.

2. Spend time to learn and become good at whatever you are choosing to *excel* in. Most people give up after a week or so of trying things out. Successful people never stop learning in order to one day become the best that they can be, as long as they know that they are on the right track.

3. Look at the results you are achieving. If your results and your vision match, continue with the actions you're taking. If they don't match, then ask yourself what changes need to be made and take action.

THE BOOK ON WINNING THE GAME OF LIFE

GAME TIME

You are on level four of the game. You are only there as a result of you having gone through levels one to three. The game does not start at level four. Where you are in the game is a result. To make it to the next level, you only have a certain time period. Your goal is to finish level four before your time is up. Having learned to use the map on the side of the screen, you formulate your plan of attack. You then also go on to gain more weapons to conquer this level. Whether you remain on level four or progress to level five will be a result that reflects on how well you are playing the game.

In what areas of your life have you been *results orientated?*

_____

_____

In what areas of your life have you not been *results orientated?* (*Be honest.*)

_____

_____

How can being results orientated help you win your game of life?

_____

_____

Take Home Message

Results are everything.
What are your results
saying about you?

05

"*The only things worth learning are the things you learn after you know it all*"

— Harry S Truman (thirty-third president of the United States)

THE TRAP

I want to start with something that I repeatedly hear unsuccessful people say: "You know, Kevin, I am just getting by." What the heck is that? There is no such thing as "getting by." You are either constantly growing or you are dying. For a while, I thought long and hard about the concept of just getting by because I used to see things as either growing or on a plateau—not dying. I mean dying sounds so negative. But the more I began to grow, the more I came to realize how true that statement was. There is no such thing as just staying the same or getting by. The world is changing at such a fast pace that, by not growing, you are falling behind others who are. Others around you will learn more skills and better utilize the resources available to them, and the more that happens, the further behind you will be.

You are either alive, or you are dead. There is no in-between.

Have you ever seen an airplane? It's either flying in the air, or it's parked in the terminal. There is no middle ground, is there?

Have you ever watched a plant over a period of time? If so, you noticed that it was either growing or dying. There was no middle ground.

Speaking of plants, let me tell you a story. My family went away for a month, and I was left in charge of taking care of the plants in our home (big mistake). Within a month of not being given the care they needed, our lovely plants were not so lovely anymore. Along with the thousands of dollars of losses I incurred, I wasn't popular in our household for a while. Plants either grow, or die. I learned this lesson the hard way. There was no middle ground.

Those who are winning the game of life are constantly growing because they know what the alternative is and choose to stay clear of it. Successful people constantly learn and grow.

"Knowledge has to be improved, challenged, and increased constantly, or it vanishes."
—Peter Drucker, influential business guru

Successful people who are winning the game of their lives have had to drop their egos to acquire this weapon. The fifth SECRET WEAPON is to constantly learn and grow. Successful people know that they will never know it all. If they were to become complacent, the people around them who were constantly growing would soon overtake them. In today's world, where many are hungry to learn and better themselves, those applying this weapon are growing faster and are operating smarter than the majority.

Choose a particular aspect of your life and write down how you improved over the last five years.

_____

_____

_____

Look at yourself and what you have achieved in the last five years. If you have accomplished a lot, then there is no way you are the same person you were five years ago. To have done well in the last five years, you must have seriously improved in your chosen field. You might very well be unhappy about where you are in life, and your rate of growth might not be where you would like to be, but, nonetheless, you have grown. The person you are today is who you have grown to be. To excel, you must constantly grow further.

If you have not learned and improved in the last five years, then your results will be a reflection of that. Only you know. You could lie to everyone else, but you can never lie to yourself. As a person, you have either grown, or you have backtracked. Again, there is no middle ground.

It's time that you pressed on the *growth accelerator.*

You must grow on a daily basis. My single biggest mistake in my earlier years was not working on my personal growth on a daily basis. This hindered the rate of my success. I thought I knew it all, and I wondered why things were not progressing at the speed that I wanted.

So how do you grow?

By surrounding yourself with the right people. If you are fortunate to be surrounded by people who are living the life you want, and have achieved what you want to achieve, then try to learn from them as much as you can. If you were like me and had no role model as such (in lifestyle success), then start reading. Read more and more books on what you need to learn to get to your destination. If you're not a reader, then grab a CD. There is a lot of information in any field that you wish to improve on to help you grow. You should have no excuse.

If you are serious about winning the game of your life, you can subscribe to my newsletters that I send out periodically to help keep you motivated and on track with what you wish to achieve. Visit www.kevinabdulrahman.com and enter your details to be on my Million Dollar Mailing List. This will entitle you to receive the articles for free.

Here's the trap:

Some people get an early break, and they start to prematurely succeed on their destination to *winning the game*. Then they fall into a trap. They make the inherent mistake of quickly coming to the conclusion that they have a complete understanding of all that they need to know. They no longer feel the need to learn. They ride the high horse named "Know it All." For anyone to ever think that they know everything is dangerous. This is the poison that has seen many crash and burn early on in their journeys, just when it looked like they had a promising future. It is a trap that many get caught up in. Those winning the game of life learn to catch themselves when they start to feel like they know everything they need to know, and they *get out of this trap quickly*.

"The moment you think that you know it all, will be the moment of your downfall."
—Socrates, philosopher of Ancient Greece

One day, I was talking to a very wealthy man in his office.

He said, "The moment you think that you know it all will be the moment you start falling off your horse."

That hit me like a ton of bricks. Here I was aspiring to win my game of life, and I was starting to do well. I was getting confident in mastering THE SECRET WEAPONS of the game, and there *was* a hint of arrogance in the back of my mind, which led me to think that I knew certain things and wouldn't need to know any more with regards to certain paths in my game. Today, I'm a lot wiser than I was in my younger days. That we don't know how much we don't know continues to amaze me.

How many times has knowing it all caught you? How many times has it caught someone you know? How many times have you veered off some proven sales scripts because you thought you knew it all, but then your results started to go backward? How many times have you decided to reinvent the wheel because you got over-confident, only to find your results become less than flattering? What people do is amazing. Many achieve the results they are aiming for in the beginning, and then, for some reason or another, they have the desire to change things. Watch out for that trap. The next time you think you might be getting on your high horse, think of how painful the fall will be coming down from this wild, know-it-all horse. For many, such a fall has spelled the end of their journey.

Back in my university days, I studied for a health sciences degree. One of the reasons I chose not to go on and study medicine was that I really didn't feel like continuing to study for so many years to come. I'd had enough, and I really didn't see myself as the type of person who would want to read books and learn for what seemed to be a lifetime. I was more of a learn-from-experience person, and spending another ten years studying seemed like a burden.. I decided to just go out there and do something that wouldn't require me to be in classroom for years to come. I enjoyed the classroom environment for a short period, but it wasn't where I wanted to be year after year.

What I didn't realize was that, to win the game of life, I would always have to be a student of the game. In fact, the people who are the best of the best at winning their games are usually the best students. I learned the hard way and realized that I would be a student for life if my intention was to *win*. Initially, it wasn't by choice but, as I saw the power in *constantly learning*, I began to love it—every single word, every single drop, every single move. Everything I learned I cherished and valued. I soaked it all up like a dry sponge in need of water. I was bettering my game. I gained that secret weapon of *constantly learning* to grow and everything I learned every day was simply sharpening that tool. Now that weapon is yours. Use it.

"The fellow who thinks he knows it all is especially annoying to those of us who do."
—Harold Coffin, humor columnist

Here is something to be aware of that will also help you to grow: When someone is talking to you, and you say, "I know" or "I've heard this already," you have subconsciously shut yourself off from learning. If you go to a seminar with the mind-set that you know everything, you will not gain from the gems being thrown out even if they land right in your hand. If you are reading this book, and you're saying to yourself, "*I know, I know, I know,*" then stop right here because the time you spend on this book will be a waste of time. Jumping on the know-it-all horse is also known as *arrogance*. Never take things for granted. Remember, every day brings about its own mysteries, and to take any day for granted is unwise. Always work on the philosophy of taking on board at least one new point every day that can help you move ahead in your life.

A word of caution: I have been caught up in this trap with my youngest brother. Being the older and wiser one (he laughed when he read this), I would never truly listen to him. In the back of my mind, I would say, "What could he possibly know that I don't?" I then realized how much he actually knew and how smart he was. If only I would have listened to his suggestions, a particular business project of ours would have flourished much sooner. I know that in numerous cultures, the older people don't listen to the youth and vice versa. I urge you to stop the madness. Keep your mind open, and you will be amazed at what you can learn from one another. Just try it. Every one of us has had different experiences in our lives, so we all have something unique to offer. Times are changing; there is so much that we must learn just to keep up.

THE SECRET WEAPONS in this book will only be exposed to the people who understand that they don't know, and will *never* know, everything. There is always room for improvement in everything we do in life. It is a never ending journey of self-discovery. Just when we think we have done something well, someone else beats you. Just when you have made the best coffee, someone else makes it better. Just when you watch a box office hit that has set a new benchmark, another one breaks it the following year. Just when you break a record, someone else breaks it shortly after. The four-minute mile was seen as an impossible barrier prior to 1954. Subsequently, more and more people broke the barrier because it became mentally possible. Just when a person under forty makes the Forbes 400 list, there are dozens more who make the list. Just look at how people have come from absolutely nowhere to being on that list—the likes of eBay founder, Pierre Omidyar, or Sergey Brin and Larry Page, the founders of Google.

The world is constantly changing and improving; so be open to learning, or you will miss the boat. Two individuals in the same city will read this book at the same time, yet they will both achieve different levels of success. Why the difference? Because one person will learn and go to work on the weapons, while the other will never take these weapons into consideration because they felt that they already knew it all.

GAME TIME

You are playing the game, and you are having a good run. Things are going your way. You are getting a handle on the game, and you are moving through it with a great deal of confidence now. You are able to speed up the pace of the game. But then you start to become arrogant in thinking that you know it all and, *whaaam*, you fall in the ditch and cost yourself a lifeline. It's a jolt, and a reminder for you to come off your high horse and pay attention to your ever-changing surroundings. We tend to have good runs when we're playing, and they get to us. It isn't until we lose a lifeline or our life level diminishes that we realize we need to move ahead with the same care, attention, and awareness of our surroundings as when we started. After all, that gave us the desired result; why not keep at it? Why let our ego take over? You might be advised by a friend who has played at the same level previously to use smarter and faster ways of completing the level. Listening to someone who has played this particular game and succeeded at it is usually a smart move. Use the cheat sheets shared by the right people whenever you can, as it will help you to get through the challenges more quickly.

Master the weapon of *constantly learning to grow*. Yes, at times it will cost you your ego, but you must realize that there is always a price to pay. You can have your ego, or you can become successful, but you can't always have both. I wanted to win the game, and if learning was the price to pay, then I had to drop my ego simply to keep up with the world, or I would be left behind.

You are in control. The choice is always yours.

How has falling into the trap of believing you already know it all affected you so far? (*Be honest.*)

_____

_____

What two things *must* you do to stay clear from this trap?

_____

_____

Take Home Message

This weapon requires you to be grounded at all times. You can't be on a high horse if you want gain it. The strike is made from the ground.

06

"*But I do nothing upon myself,
and yet I am my own executioner*"

– John Donne (ingenious poet)

YOUR WORST ENEMY

You are working hard, you are learning every day, and of course you have challenges as you progress. You are trying your hardest, and as you do so, things start to get easier over time.

If you are in business, things start to click for you, and you start to generate sales. You start to do well, and you are now riding the tidal wave heading toward success.

Then one fine day, you realize that things have been stagnant over the last few weeks, but you think nothing of it. Maybe it was the weather. Months later you ask yourself, "What is going on? Why am I not growing? I'm doing all the right things." (So you think.) "And yet I'm not getting the results."

You start thinking of why you are not doing well, and since you are not getting the right results, your reasons seem to come flying in the door. You ask yourself, "Who are my worst enemies? What is holding me back?"

Is it the naysayers? Is it the people who always put you down? Is it those who put doubt in your mind? Is it the economic conditions? Is it the weather? Is it the fact that you're having family problems? What is it? Who is your worst enemy?

Your questioning drags on until the day comes when you just pull the plug on whatever it is you're doing. If it's a relationship, you pull out of it. If it's a friendship, you create the friction that makes it fall apart. If it's a business project, you simply give up on it.

Who is your biggest and worst enemy? Your worst enemy is unveiled: It's *you*.

You have become your biggest hindrance.

Welcome to the world of *self-sabotage*. Self-sabotage is the unique ability we possess to impair ourselves and do a great job of killing our own growth and happiness. It sounds bizarre, and it took me a few years until I truly experienced and understood the concept. From then on, it was frightening to notice the people around me doing it in some shape or form. I realized that many people experience self-sabotage, and only the few who are successful survive it.

I was very sad to see a good friend of mine go through this process. We were very close, and at the end of it all, he had lost his business, his reputation, his integrity, and the one thing that mattered the most to me—our friendship. He was a very hard worker and had a lot of challenges working his way up. He got to a point where he thought he knew it all. He wouldn't do the little things he did earlier on in his business that contributed to his success. As a result, he took a dive, and he was finding it hard to make ends meet. Then self-sabotage got him by the neck. He started making up all kinds of stories to explain why things weren't going right. He was quick to point his trigger finger to those closest to him, and unfortunately, in the end, he suffered. It was very sad to see.

The reality is this: We all do it.

We all sabotage ourselves, but the majority of people do so a lot. In high doses this is equivalent to committing *suicide*, metaphorically speaking.

In my talks, I always tell people to simply, "Get over yourself, and get on with it." Most people's biggest stumbling block is not other individuals; it's not the environment; nor is it the weather. It isn't the economy or the naysayers. Indeed, it is themselves. They are prisoners of their own making. They are prisoners of their minds. They are chained to the corner of their mind's cells. They took the chain and voluntarily locked themselves up. And since they've locked themselves up, only they possess the key to their freedom.

GAME TIME

You are now in a place that is booby-trapped with land mines. Initially, you might be unaware of the mines, until a friend tells you about them. Now that you know they're there, it would be stupid and dangerous to walk straight into a mine because, guess what happens, *you get blown to pieces!* Some, who are tired of playing, throw in the towel and simply walk into the booby trap to end the game. That's self-sabotage. We have all done it at some point when we've decided that we've had enough. But those who are serious about winning this level stay away from the traps, jump over the visible land mines, and get to the end. To them, the game is worth playing for the reward of winning.

So how do we prevent *self-sabotage?*

How do those who are winning the game of life make it to the finish line? What secret weapon have they acquired and mastered to conquer self sabotage? The sixth SECRET WEAPON acquired and mastered by those winning their game of life is *controlling their inner dialogue.* I mean that dialogue you have with yourself.

"Thought is the sculptor who can create the person you want to be."
—Henry David Thoreau, poet and philosopher

Do you know people who talk to themselves? We all do.

I want you to think of your current situation. Now, let's say that I suggest that you attend a five thousand-dollar workshop, one that will help you gain the knowledge to double your income in twelve months.

What thoughts are going through your mind?

Write out your inner dialogue. For example, write, "Oh that's too expensive" or "I don't have the time."

What story is going through your head?

_____

_____

_____

Time and time again, it saddens me to see capable athletes, worthy of representing their countries, held back by their inner dialogue. It didn't matter how much potential I saw in them, they held themselves back. They did not compete at the top level when they could have because they did not *control their inner dialogue*. They didn't see it in themselves to stretch further and make it *big*. The same applies to people in friendships and relationships, personal and in business. A lot of friendships and relationships are, unfortunately, ended due to the inner dialogue that individuals have with themselves. You could be late for dinner one night, and your spouse could have an inner dialogue that says, "You don't care about me anymore." You were just told that you had to have a work project in by 6:00 p.m., and you had to make it happen. You didn't think being on time for dinner was a big deal, but it was to your spouse. How many times have you heard of people having arguments in business? Their inner dialogue is, unfortunately, dictating their actions. If only people would *control their inner dialogue* and communicate their thoughts clearly to one another, then all the friction and confusion would disappear.

I want to share with you a friend's experience, as I feel it applies to most of us. You may find a trigger in her story to help you deal with your stories that you might make up.

This young lady was twenty-one at the time, and I had known her for a while. She had been involved with a network marketing company for less than a year when she felt that she had reached a plateau in the expansion of her business. Going through her skill set, we concluded (or I should say, I suggested) she should buy some qualified leads and start making calls so that she could generate more appointments. She agreed to the suggestion with excitement, knowing that she could get a lot more business that way since she was very strong on the phone. Talking to strangers was like a walk in the park for her because of the work experience she had. So now I was thinking that this young lady would have her business boom in the next ninety days.

Guess what happened?

Nothing ... nothing happened—nil, zip, nada, nothing.

Ninety days later, I asked her, "What happened? Didn't we agree that buying those leads would help build your business?"

Her reply was, "Yes"

So I asked again, "What happened?"

This young lady, wrote me a note detailing exactly what went through her mind when we had a solution that would help in building her business.

In her words, she said, "Kevin told me to buy some leads. The idea excited me. First, I pictured what would be possible and what could come out of it in terms of my success. Then it went *dark*. At a million miles an hour, fears flooded into my mind, and I found myself mumbling, 'What happens if I get lots of appointments and then don't have time to fit them around my current day job? Should I maybe wait until I quit my job? Oh but if it doesn't go to plan, I will be financially stuck. Oh maybe I will just flag the idea.'"

Now isn't that fascinating?

I asked her to read what she had written out loud. This young lady couldn't help but laugh at what she'd written. Isn't it funny that we all do this in some shape and form. The inner dialogue we have, the stories we make up—it's amazing how often we are our own worst enemy.

In the case of my friend, her fears were *made up*. She didn't control her inner dialogue and, hence, made up her story. She read what she had written for a second time and realized that she could control how she thought. If she was going to make up a story, why not make it a good one?

Now go back and reread the story you wrote to yourself about attending the five thousand-dollar workshop. Could it possibly sound funny?

Is it a made-up story? Just think of what your inner dialogue is costing you.

What is it costing you when you shortchange yourself due to your *inner dialogue*? What did it cost my friend?

When I was acquiring my secret weapons, I attended many seminars. I would pay whatever the asking price was if I wanted to gain and master a particular skill set. I remember catching up with friends and, with eagerness, telling them that I'd just paid ten thousand dollars of my hard earned money for a three-day seminar. They would all look at me in disbelief, and some would even say I was wasting my money.

In my head, I was saying, "Ten thousand dollars is nothing to learn the recipe of how Mr. X has created his success. Once I learn and practice what he has done, I'll be able to make my money back over and over again." On the other hand, my friend had this go through his head (I know because he was blatantly clear about what he meant): "Why would you waste ten thousand dollars on a seminar?"

Can you see how the two inner dialogues could lead to a different quality of life? I can tell you personally that those friends are all in the same position in life that they were in a few years ago, while my life has catapulted—not because I am special, but because I mastered *controlling my inner dialogue*.

Part of my inner dialogue was also to learn to ask good questions when coming across a challenging situation. Most people ask, "Why is this happening to me? Why is it always me?" I learned to control my inner dialogue and to have a successful person's inner dialogue. I learned to stop whining. I decided to drop any story I could potentially make up and say, "How can I get around this? What opportunities are here because of this?"

The quality of your life is dependent on the quality of questions you ask yourself. Could you then control and, hence, change your inner dialogue? Can you see the difference changing your dialogue could make in your results? In order to become mentally tough and control what goes through your mind, you simply need to make a snap decision to have an inner dialogue similar to those who are successful in the aspect of life you are interested in.

Once you've unlocked your ability to control your mind (and this will come with practice), you will be a force not to be reckoned with. It is time you unleashed the animal within you.

Now that you are aware of your inner dialogue, practice *controlling* it. Always listen to yourself and ask, "Is this talk conducive to helping me *win the game of my life?*"

I shared this with the young lady I previously mentioned, and she told me what her inner dialogue was this time around.

"I could make the appointments and make the money or not bother and stay comfortable where I am now. But what changes? One way means that I could potentially move forward, and the other way means I can stay where I am now. Convincing myself is comfortable, but it can't be that comfortable if I am searching for ways to escape my current reality. Either way, like you always say, Kevin, I am always paying the price."

GAME TIME

In the game, does your character have any thoughts? If you were to press the *down* button, does the character look to the left? Does the character scratch his or her head and say, "Gee, I'm not sure if I want to do that"? Or does he or she simply follow the command you pushed on the controller button? The game is played with no withholding inner dialogue. The eye is on the prize, and the motion is forward. Apply the same in your life.

If anything, as the gamer, your inner dialogue goes something like this: *"Bring it; I'm burning hot."* Apply the same in your life.

"Watch your thoughts, for they become words.
Watch your words, for they become actions.
Watch your actions, for they become habits.
Watch your habits, for they become character.
Watch your character, for it becomes your destiny."
—Anonymous

THE STORIES WE MAKE UP

I was watching a movie that had this grump character in it. As the story unfolded, it was sad to find out that the guy, who always wanted to be a father, was told that he could not have any children. The guy received the sad news and decided to make up a story in his head that the world was against him. He made up a story that his brother was better than him because he had a child. He made up a story that his wife would leave him for someone else, since she wanted to be a mother. This just went on and on. Finally, his younger brother helped him realize that everything he was doing and acting upon was based on stories he had made up in his head. They weren't facts; they were merely made up stories. His wife had no intention of leaving him.

How many times have you made up a story or two in your Mind, whether it was regarding friends, your significant other, associates in business, or even strangers? How many times have you passed judgments on people without knowing their true intentions? How many times have you made assumptions without asking direct questions and getting direct answers?

At times, we dwell upon these made-up stories for so long that, unfortunately, they become living realities. Everything you have or will have started or will start as a thought in your mind. Everything that has materialized in your life has, in one way or another, started as a tiny thought.

You must start seeing yourself as a success. If you are going to imagine and assume, then you might as well imagine and assume that you'll do well in life. Successful people expect to do well. They envision success and expect to get what they are working toward. By visualizing the things you want, you will make it easier for yourself to get there. Once you are there in your mind, the rest will follow.

At certain stages in life, we feel that things are unbearable and impossible. It is such a pity to see the number of times people have talked themselves out of a great idea or business venture. Everything you desire in life is possible—*everything.*

Adidas summed it nicely: *"Impossible is nothing."*

So simple, so brief—these are three words to always remember when you're dealing with life.

Recently I have realized the correlation between one's inner dialogue and the term *beginner's luck.* I wanted to understand why this holds true in many aspects of life. I thought of how there are things I would think twice about these days as compared to the times when I would take so-called risks—all because I have been exposed to more. It made me realize that the only reason I did well out of a venture when I was rather naïve in the game of success was because I was just that—*naïve.* I didn't know much, and I didn't have people around me telling me what I could or couldn't do. I had a stronger inner dialogue that said, "Hey, I've got to do what I've got to do." So I did, and I did well.

"The happiest person is the person who thinks the most interesting thoughts."
—Timothy Dwight, eighteenth-century poet and writer

Get down to business and give everything you want in life a proper shot. Here is a way I control my inner dialogue: I use the following catchphrase every time I'm faced with a stumbling block, *"Bring it; I'm burning hot."* I say it in a way that my mind believes it. It resets my *inner dialogue* and takes me to a state of power and action. Feel free to use it if it sits well with you. Once you master this weapon, your worst enemy will become your best friend.

What has your *inner dialogue* been like so far? (*Be honest.*)

_____

_____

What two positive statements can you make to *control your inner dialogue* and take it to a state of power?

_____

_____

Take Home Message

If you are going to make up a story in your head, you may as well make one that's positive—one in which you get everything you want.

07

*"There are no mental jobs,
only mental attitudes"*

- William Bennett (Politician)

WHICH OF THE TWO ARE YOU?

I used to sell alarms door-to-door. We would have a daily team meeting at 1:00 p.m. and hit the road at 2:00 p.m. to start knocking on doors. On one particular day, I was pretty down and didn't feel like being at work. I just wasn't in the swing of things, and work was the last thing on my mind. As I was about to leave our sales van, my friend said, "Kevin, come here. I want to show you something."

He wrote out on a piece of paper: "A . T . T . I . T . U . D . E."

Unenthused, I just shrugged and said, "Yeah, it says attitude, so what?"

He placed his hand on my left shoulder, looked me in the eye, and said, "I want you to leave now, but before you knock on your first door, replace every letter in *attitude* with the number in its alphabetical position (for example, A=1, T=20). Once you have done that, add all the numbers together.

Instead of leaving and working it out in my head, I went to the back of the sales van, got my pen, and started to work it out right then and there.

A=1, T=20, T=20, I=9, T=20, U=21, D=5, E=4

1+20+20+9+20+21+5+4=100

I looked up and said, "one hundred." He then said, "That's how important your attitude is." A 100 percent attitude was important if I was going to spend my day working. He said that I was wasting my time being there if I wasn't going to have a 100 percent attitude. Today I look back and thank him for that great piece of advice. A powerful secret weapon had just landed in my lap.

With what attitude are you playing the game of your life?

Are you a can't-do-this and can't-do-that person?

Or are you someone who looks at all stumbling blocks and asks, "How can I overcome this, one way or another?"

Do you see the cup half full or half empty?

Or maybe you are a person who will grab a jug of water, fill up the cup, and say, "Now it's a full cup."

Do you look at a situation and say, "How can I make it work?" Or do you just decide, "We have a problem, and I can't do much about it"? Do you take control? Or do you give up?

Can you look up in to the sky when you are facing down? Your attitude will determine your altitude in life. If you are coming from an attitude of negativity, the direction you will see is down. If you were to only look at one side of the coin, does that mean the other side doesn't exist? Of course not. You may simply be choosing not to look at the other side.

Successful people who win the game of life have acquired and mastered the seventh SECRET WEAPON: a *how-can-I-do-it?* attitude.

"They can because they think they can."
—Virgil, poet

Do the fishes stop swimming simply because the water conditions get rough? Do they stop swimming because people are fishing? Do professional athletes stop playing their game because they are not ahead of their game in the first half? Does a mother give up on a child simply because her little one is slow to walk? All successful people see through the tough times in order to win their game of life. They are always asking, "How can I do it?"

So how can you do it?

Most people think about what they can't do all the time. If you keep on doing that, you will end up being like the majority of people. Doing what the majority does will result in you having what the majority has. Do you want what most people have?

I've spoken with thousands of successful people, and they've all said that, in many instances, they had no idea how they were going to win their game but didn't let that hold them down. They just knew that they were playing to win, and they'd figure out the "how-to" along the way. Most people spend most of their time worrying about how they won't be able to succeed. You give a recommendation to help them with their challenge, and they are quick to reply with concerns as to how and why they can't do it, rather than thinking, "*How can I do it?* How can I make it happen?"

You start a project—launching a new business, learning to play a musical instrument, playing a sport, or getting a degree, to name a few. You are all excited at first, but then you come across a stumbling block. You get annoyed, then frustrated, then depressed, and then you give up. What have you achieved? *Nothing.* Should you receive a medal for it? There will always be challenges in life, so you'd better start thinking about how they can be smartly overcome or used in your favor. By asking, how can I do it, you are orientated toward finding a solution rather than focusing on the problem. Don't play victim; be a victor. Choose to be a *winner.*

It's not what happens to you that matters; rather, what you do when things happen is what's important. Do you think that a winner might have a different attitude when confronted with situations than those who don't make it? *Absolutely.*

To be a winner, you must first have a winner's how-can-I-do-it attitude. Most people say that, when things get better, their attitude will change. I am here to tell you that, until you acquire and master the powerful weapon that is a *how-can-I-*

do-it attitude, things will be the same. The change needs to come from you first. Make the move. Start instilling and practicing a winning attitude, and you will start to win the game of life.

As long as you always get up one time more than you fall, you will still be standing, won't you? You don't have a chance of winning if you remain on your back. Can you win a boxing match with your back on the mat? The only way to win is to get back up again and stand another chance. The only way to win is to ask, "*How can I do this?*" How can I land my K.O.

So if you have been lying down from a previous hit, use what you are reading right now and choose to *stand up*. Stand up and smile at adversities because you owe it to yourself to live a full life. You want to be able to look back and be proud of the 100 percent attitude that led to you living a full 100 percent life.

GAME TIME

Your attitude is right. You're playing to win. You will come across challenges throughout the level. If your mind is set on getting through the level, you will get through it You could be losing game lives, but you are not fazed because you know your friend played this very game and managed to get through. You know that if he or she did it, you can do it too. You have this big grin on your face, even though you are going through challenging times. You have a point to make, so you play on with that winning attitude. If you know you are going to win anyway, it becomes only a matter of time until you get through the level. You will always be proven right if you hold on to your winning attitude.

I want to share with you the story of this young boy from whom I learned a very valuable lesson. I was at a church a few years ago, mourning the death of my friend's father. Everyone was quiet, and I was watching some children play outside. I couldn't help but see a ledge that they were running over, back and forth, and thinking to myself that it was not safe; it was only a matter of time before one of them would fall flat smack on their face. Sure enough, within a few seconds, one of the children fell smack on his face. He hit the floor so hard it made me cringe.

Now this is what the young boy did:

He got up and started looking around for attention, but because everyone was so busy with the funeral, he realized that he was not going to get any attention. He shook himself off, ran toward the kids, and continued to play with a great smile on his face. It was as if nothing had happened. I remember simply thinking, *wow*.

The kids kept running in and out of the church and what do you know … *smack*; the same boy hit the ground face first again. Now I was thinking that surely this would be a full-blown cry, enough to interrupt the funeral from proceeding. But no, he got up, noticed that no one was looking, shrugged himself off, and continued to play with his friends. This time, he had an even bigger smile on his face. I was amazed, to say the least, but I learned something very valuable that day. I learned to develop that young boy's attitude—a winning one. He applied the *how-can-I-do-it* attitude by getting up after each fall. He knew that having his face on the floor would not allow him to have the fun he wanted to have with his friends. He knew from such a tender age that he needed to pick himself up and continue playing. If only more of us had that young boy's attitude! Unfortunately, this attitude diminishes in many of us as we grow older. We take all the negative comments from our surroundings to heart and start listening to what other people have to say. We start listening to people who have their set of limitations and who don't have what we want, but tell us what we can and can't do in life. As a result, we get tired of picking ourselves up.

Last time I checked, none of these people will provide for your family or put food on your table. None of them will provide you with what you desire in life on any level. Think like a winner and never allow yourself to drop your attitude. You will never see a truly successful person have a negative attitude. People with winning attitudes are always solution orientated, asking, "*How can I do it?*" And they are always the ones getting the desired results. Why?

Because their attitude adds up to 100 percent.

Think of two occasions where you did not have a 100 percent attitude? How did it affect you? (*Be honest.*)

_____

_____

What two winning attitudes could you add to your arsenal?

_____

_____

Take Home Message

Always ask, "How does a
winner go about doing this?"
Remember the young boy.

08

"I have missed more than nine thousand shots in my career. I have lost almost three hundred games. On twenty-six occasions, I have been entrusted to take the game's winning shot, and I missed. I have failed over and over and over again in my life. And that is precisely why I succeed"

— *Michael Jordan (greatest basketball player of all time)*

HOW TO BECOME A DIAMOND

First of all, you don't get a medal for giving up. Anyone can give up. "I *gave up* when things got challenging" won't make much of a significant story for your memoirs. How many people are remembered for giving up? How many people are rewarded for giving up? You reap the rewards by hanging in there and doing all the right things, even when the going gets tough.

I once heard that the reason a butterfly gets its beautiful wings is because of the struggle it goes through to come out of its chrysalis. It's because of this struggle that it ends up emerging as a beautiful creature.

Do you know of anyone who wanted to achieve a higher muscle mass and managed to do so with absolutely no weight training? Would it be fair to say that you need to lift some weight to start building more muscle? Can you increase your muscle mass if you don't have any form of resistance training?

It would be ridiculous to even think that. To develop muscles, you must lift weights. No weights means no resistance. No resistance means no growth.

Successful people have acquired and mastered the eighth SECRET WEAPON: *being persistent*. The majority of people stop at the early stages of resistance. That's why they stop growing. Successful people understand that, if they're not faced with resistance of some sort, then they're not growing. They simply regard resistance from the stumbling blocks they encounter as the weight training they need to do. To grow and become successful requires the *persistence* to outlast the resistance. Not one successful person can go through the journey of winning his or her game in life without mastering this weapon.

I have a few friends who are great body sculptors. They work very hard to get the bodies they have. To achieve those bodies, they have worked out rigorously and kept to a strict nutrition plan. These friends I was referring to have all told me, repeatedly, that they still have days when they simply don't feel like working out. Yet, they work out anyway. I remember a friend once saying, "Kevin, I would much rather sit at home and watch a movie than go for a forty-five minute run at night in the cold weather." But because they are so focused about their results, they never ever, ever, ever give up. They hang in for the ultimate pleasure of winning their game of life.

Is it worth it in the end? Well, you would have to ask them, but from what I have found from successful people in any field, the common response is, "Absolutely!" These friends of mine have bodies most people envy but only the elite few who have learned the discipline of persistence can achieve. The same applies to every aspect of your life. Master this weapon and you can have what ever you want in life.

If you don't want to face the resistance, you will have *no chance* of winning. Resistance is part of the game. You have to do your weight training.

Learn to accept it. Learn to love it.

Learn to outlast the resistance.

GAME TIME

Have you ever played a game where you simply cruised right through the level with no challenges on the way? It would be pointless. The game would be boring, and you wouldn't spend the best of two minutes playing if there wasn't a challenge. Instead, what makes it exciting is that we are constantly faced with challenges and *bad guys* to defeat. We could be losing game lives, but with every challenge we face, we acquire new skills and polish our techniques. As gamers, we keep at it, and, sooner or later, we figure out how to demolish the opposition and advance to the next level. We could spend endless game lives and hours at a time to cross one level. Because we hang in, every time we lose a life, all we have to do is be ready to go again as soon as the character reappears on the screen. We have unlimited chances if we choose to be persistent. Nothing gives us more satisfaction than the triumph of completing a tough level after trying for so long. That breakthrough feeling is addictive.

"Great works are performed, not by strength, but by perseverance."
—Samuel Johnson, eighteenth-century English writer

Imagine the Rugby World Cup final.

Do you think the elite players on both teams have the total intention to play for the full eighty minutes? Imagine watching the All Blacks play against England, and fifteen minutes into the game, the score is 12 – 0 against the All Blacks, so they quit. How often do you see the losing team throw in the towel and call it quits? How often do you see a team walk out halfway through the game, saying, "We've had enough. We'll be at the local pub. Join us for a few drinks"? Now you might see that in amateur players and, hence, they're not playing at the top level, but you will *never* see an elite athlete or an elite team do that. They always play the game to the end. They play a full game, giving blood, sweat, and tears all the way.

No team has ever won a gold medal by pulling out and not finishing the rugby world cup final. The players must hang in and play for the full eighty minutes to have a chance at winning. *Persistence* is a tough secret weapon to master. You need to practice constantly to develop this weapon. Most people don't ever develop this weapon because most people pull out fifteen minutes into an eighty-minute game.

How many times have we seen teams trailing behind for the majority of the game only to come back and win by scoring in the last few minutes, even in the last few seconds? The same applies to whatever aspect of your life you're focusing on. Don't let challenges in the first day, week, month, or year stop you from winning the game. Don't let them stop you from living life to its fullest. In life, it's never over until you quit. Only when you quit do you lose any chance of making it. It may seem that you are losing in the early minutes, but play the *full* game. Success is inevitable when you play till the end.

"I always win because I never quit."
—Kevin Abdulrahman

I want you to think of the shiny gems loved by women, also known as their best friends, diamonds. Beautiful, sparkling, and pleasing to the eye, these diamonds were once black coals—the same black coals that were once ugly, dull, and unpleasant to look at. After being under immense pressure, some coals crack. Those that crack do not become diamonds. Only the coals that withstand pressure over time end up becoming the precious diamonds.

So whenever you feel like giving up, ask yourself, "Will I remain a dull and ugly piece of coal? Or will I become a bright, shining *diamond*?"

"Success seems to be largely a matter of hanging on after others have let go."
—William Feather, author and publisher

What can you say about your level of persistence in life? (*Be honest.*)

_____

_____

What two things *must* you do to help you become a diamond?

_____

_____

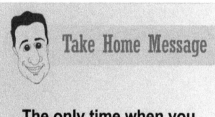

Take Home Message

The only time when you truly fail is when you quit. Choose to become a diamond.

09

"What would you attempt to do if you knew you would not fail?"

-Robert Schuller (Televangelist and pastor)

WHAT IF FAILURE WAS NOT AN OPTION?

I had written the script for a CD one of my companies was producing. It was my first script and an unknown territory for me back then. It was a ten-minute track with the script all written out, rehearsed, and even recorded as a draft. What we needed to do was to professionally record it in a studio, an hour-long process; take it for a few hours of editing by a sound engineer; and then have a company mass produce the CD professionally—a process that ended up totaling no more than six hours. It was done and here I was finally picking it up. The six-hour process had taken me over six months to complete. Why? What happened?

Was it the guys who were producing the CD? Did their stamping plant get damaged in a fire? Did the sound engineer make a mistake and required me to re-record everything? Did I lose the script, taking me six months to recall all the material that was to be on the CD? No, it was none of that.

It was me! For one reason or another, there was something that held me back. Remember that I talked about controlling your inner dialogue? Well that played a big part. My inner dialogue was obviously in disagreement with what I needed to achieve. I had to work on becoming aware of it and changing it to align with where I wanted to be in life. There was this little feeling holding me back—this all too familiar feeling that stops the majority of people from achieving great things in life.

What is stopping you?

It can only be summed up as one thing:

F · E · A · R

an enemy that we create and that holds us back. But is it really as big as what we make it out to be?

Whether it is *fear* of failure, *fear* of what other people think, *fear* of ridicule, you name it, there is a *fear* for everything. This isn't something I want to dwell on, but the reality is that we all have some sort of *fear* to face. What the fear is depends on the time and situation you are in. I want to focus on a particular fear that stops people from even starting most things. It is the fear of failure. Most people fear what would happen if they fail before having even started on their task. I have experienced this fear many times myself, and it's something I see many struggle with.

But what if you knew for sure that there was no chance of failure? What if success was guaranteed? Would you do what you need to do to achieve the lifestyle of your dreams? If you knew that there was no chance of failure, what would you be doing differently in your life? If success was guaranteed, would you follow and do what other successful people do? If you knew that success was a recipe that, once learned, ensures that anyone can bake the cake of success, would you start that new business venture? What so-called risks would you take? Would you get a better job? Would you go for that promotion? Would you open up to your loved ones? Would you *dare to dream*, all knowing that you have no chance of failing?

"Failure is not an option. Everyone has to succeed."
—Arnold Schwarzenegger, (Mr. Olympia, a Hollywood hero and Governor of California)

If success was guaranteed, would you feel any fear or doubt? Would you still be scared? If you think about it, you wouldn't have a reason *not* to take action. Successful people have developed and mastered the ninth SECRET WEAPON: *having the end reward in mind.* They weigh up risks, costs, effort, and time with the *end reward in mind.* This sets them in the mind-set of being reward focused, giving them the belief necessary for them to do what they wish to do. They have the end reward in sight. The process they go through to get to that end is like a movie. What matters is how this movie ends. You can go through rough times, yet you know that, when all is said and done, it is the end reward that matters. I personally like movies with happy endings, and nothing annoys me more than good movies with sad endings. It just kills the movie for me. The happy ending is the end reward you must focus on. All that really matters is how the movie ends for you in your game of life.

Most people are too scared to leap into a new business venture or take up the hobby they've always wanted or ask that someone they like out on a date. They are so worried that they will fail and not get the result they want. They don't look at the end reward; rather, they focus on all the things that could go wrong in the meantime (the least you can do is wait for a problem to arise before you worry about it). While most people focus on the risk they are taking, successful people focus on the end reward—what their actions could bring them. Not acting on your goals will give you no end result at all. That is a 100 percent guarantee. At least when you give something a go, you have a fifty-fifty chance of winning. With action, the odds of a positive result are much higher from the word *go* than if you do nothing. Remember, doing something is better than doing nothing.

If you were given two choices—(a) to do *nothing* and be guaranteed to get nothing or(b) to do *something* and have a fifty-fifty chance of achieving—wouldn't the better choice be blatantly obvious?

Most people focus on what can go wrong. Why would you want to do that? Focusing on what can go wrong has no positive impact on your life whatsoever. Focusing on it brings about *fear.* This fear builds up in people, to a point where they end up doing the all-so-familiar nothing. Think of how many times this has happened to you in your lifetime. What sort of positive impact has it had in your life? What would your life be like if you had acted upon a thought or opportunity that was presented to you in the past? How would your life be different today?

What you focus on becomes your reality. How about focusing on how things can go right? How about focusing on seeing yourself overcome any challenge that heads your way?

Learn to take your emotions out of situations, and don't be influenced by hype and media. People let their emotions dictate their actions and, since the media is filled with bad news, people end up doing nothing out of fear. By keeping your emotions at bay, you will be able to control yourself and never allow fear to prevail in your life.

GAME TIME

When was the last time you were scared to play a game? When did fear ever grip you enough to stop playing a game? Because you are playing "a game," you have no fear whatsoever. When you are playing a game, you only see challenges, setbacks, and stumbling blocks. You could be anxious at times, but the term "failure" doesn't cross your mind. You learn to get over the stumbling blocks by trying over and over again until you get past the challenge. The key is to just play. You know that you can't lose if you simply keep playing. If you just sit and stare at the screen, your character won't move, and you will be in the same place an hour down the track. There is no reward in that. You must make a move and play, focusing on the end reward of completing the level.

On many occasions, we don't even know we are fearful. After all, who wants to admit that they have fears? What would people think and say?

Who cares?!!!

It is only when we look back in time that we realize our inaction has been based on the fears we have had. What is the point of living a life that is unfulfilled, unachieved, and devoid of any excitement? That would be a miserable definition of existence. We come with nothing into this world, and we certainly leave with nothing. We have nothing to lose. What is the worst-case scenario for failing? What is the worst-case scenario for *you* failing?

You will go back to where you started! How bad can it be?

You are either living the life you fear now, or you have been at some point. So it is not unfamiliar territory. It wouldn't be that much of a discomfort to come back. You have nothing to lose and everything to gain.

"Failure? I never encountered it. All I ever met were temporary setbacks."
—Dottie Walters, renowned author and speaker

Earlier, I touched on the fact that there are always stumbling blocks in whatever you may decide to do. To hope for a totally smooth ride would be absurd. But the setbacks along the way are just temporary stumbling blocks. By no means will anything be permanent. If you keep at it, success will be yours. You must simply look at setbacks as checkpoints.

If you're going through life without setbacks, then you are not truly living to your full potential. Part of any growth or success is to experience setbacks along the way. Setbacks that make you think smarter, think harder, setbacks to help ground you if success starts to go to your head. While average people see setbacks as failures, successful people know that they are merely challenges to stretch and increase their abilities. Setbacks are the resistance needed to help you grow. One analogy I like to use is the traffic lights on the road. If you are going to visit a friend's place for dinner, chances are you will be brought to a complete halt several times due to traffic lights. It doesn't mean you won't get to your friend's place; rather you must attend to this situation (in this case wait for the light to turn green). Seeing stumbling blocks as red traffic lights will help you focus on the end reward; after all, the traffic lights never stay red forever, do they?

So many people are faced with similar situations, yet there are always different outcomes. Imagine that a group of people is each faced with the prospect of starting up a smart business. For the sake of this example, we'll say that none of them have the full capital required to do so. Some will come back and give all the reasons in the world as to why they did not start the business. They'll give you every excuse under the sun as to why they did not get the *result*. Most will tell you that they tried to be creative, they tried to look at different avenues, they had ten different options, all of which were rejected, and that's why they never started this fruitful business venture.

And then we have the people who find the full capital to start the business venture. How? The right question would really be *why*? They set their minds on the end reward and persisted by plowing through all stumbling blocks or rejections because stopping at a traffic light was not the end reward. Their destination was to start their business. And so they kept at it until they got there. They practiced and used the secret weapons we discussed in the earlier chapters.

What ten things would you do if you knew that failure was not an option?

_____

_____

_____

_____

_____

_____

_____

_____

_____

It's time you started acting on at least one of the ten things you have written down. I want to personally hear of your success. Post your success stories by jumping on www.thisisTHEBOOK.com and click on the "Share your success" button. Alternatively send my team an email with your success story on info@kevinabdulrahman.com

At certain stages in life, we feel that things are unbearable and impossible. There is no such thing.

Remember the Adidas slogan: "Impossible is *nothing.*" Always remember that phrase when you are playing the game of life. Everything you desire in life is possible—absolutely everything.

If you let fear take over, then all you'll be left with is regret. You must work out the price you have to pay to face your fear, compared to the price of living your life with regret.

I was talking to a very wealthy friend once and he told me,

"Kevin, I have made a lot of mistakes in life. I've made a lot of money, and I've lost a lot of money. I've made smart moves, and I've made stupid moves. I've taken smart risks, and I've taken silly risks. I've had great friendships, and I've ruined relationships because of my mistakes. If I could live my life again, I would do it all over again. I do not regret the mistakes at all. For the good and the bad, my only regrets in life are for the things I did not do."

I thought I had misheard him, so I said, "Pardon?

Your only regrets in life are for the things you did not do?"

He clarified; "I regret not starting the business opportunity I was presented with. I regret not saying 'I love you' to the people I cared about the most. I regret not having spent more time with my family. I regret the things I did not do."

He told me to go home and think about all the things I regretted so far in life. I couldn't sleep that night twisting and turning in bed trying to think of all the times I regretted. I realized that my friend was right; my only regrets were the things I didn't do. I remember waking up in the morning and thinking only of this statement.

"You can laugh at your past failures, but you can't laugh at your past regrets."
—Kevin Abdulrahman

Name two failures in your past that today you can laugh out loud at?

_____

_____

What two things *must* you do to help you move toward winning your game of life?

_____

_____

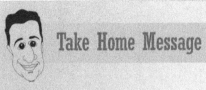

All that matters is how your movie ends.

10

*"Goals provide the energy source
that powers our lives"*

-Denis Waitley (one of America's most respected
authors, keynote lecturers, and productivity
consultants on high performance human achievement)

DO PEOPLE FEEL YOUR HEAT?

LAST-MINUTE INSERT: As I'm sitting back and reading this chapter having my latte, I have come to a realization. I am sitting in a very funky café across the road from the water, with the sun shining down, whilst I'm contemplating how to put these chapters together in an easy flow format for you to read.

It has just hit me. I have always dreamed of being a guy who could produce an international best-seller and, right now, I can say that I'm on my way to living one of my dreams of being an international bestselling author—another goal on my checklist, one that, in all honesty, I had no idea how, when, or if I would be able to achieve. I just knew that I wanted to do it. Achieving this goal, I knew, would bring me immense happiness. That was my why— my reason. The how-to I never knew. I didn't know how I'd go about doing it. It really didn't matter; somehow I would get there.

Indeed, the feeling is nice. In fact I'm in a bit of a shock. I can't help but smile away having just realized I can tick off another one of my dreams coming to reality. Funnily enough, all of my goals and dreams have just come about like that. I justt know I want it, but initially I never know how. Things just seem to fall into place if you do the right things. I am sharing this with you in order to help you see that you should dream freely. Dream of whatever you wish to be and do. No matter how crazy your dream is, no matter what other people tell you is possible or not, have no boundaries when you're dreaming. If you want it badly, and if you do the right things and persevere, you will get there.

Can you find your way home if you're hungry?

We are all different, which is what makes life so interesting. We have different dreams and goals, which stem from our desires. The reason I would do something is not the same reason you would do it. We all want to win the game of our lives in order to fulfill our particular needs. We all have goals and dreams. But what is the underlying driver?

Successful people have mastered the tenth SECRET WEAPON: having *a burning desire* to achieve their goals and dreams. They have a strong *why*. Most of the time they have no idea *how* things are supposed to happen, but their focus is not on the method. Their intention is clear and solid. Once they have made up their minds, they move forward with the end reward in mind. Because of the strength of their *desire*, they come across the answers they need along the way, throughout their journey. I'm not talking about wishful thinking. I'm talking about a strong desire—a burning one, so much so that people around can feel your heat. In my talks, I sometimes throw out the question, "Who wouldn't want to retire early? Who wouldn't want to have a great family life? Who wouldn't want to have no financial worries?" The answer is no one. So why do the majority fail? Because their desire is wishy-washy. Their desire is shaky and, hence, easily influenced by the environment in which they live.

Another reason most people become stuck is that they're so worried about how to do something that they lose the focus of their desire. They are so focused on the method of getting there that, when a challenge arises, their desire fades. They feel that, just because the path to their goal is blocked, they should let go of their dream. For this reason, they never get started.

Many of us do this without realizing it. By focusing on your strong desire, you won't be worried about the how-tos. It is said that 80 percent of all success stems from a strong desire, and only 20 percent is the how-to. Ask any successful person and they will confirm it with you.

Let me show you an example. Imagine you have just finished work. You're rather hungry and, driving down the road heading home, you realize that the route home is blocked by road works. The way home is closed. Does that mean you give up on getting home? Would you simply park your car to one side and sleep in the car for the night, hungry until the next day?

You find another route to get home, don't you? Why?

Because you are not focused on the process or the possibility of getting lost. Your strong desire is to get home so that you can eat and rest, and you get there every single time.

"Where there is hunger, there is a way."
—Kevin Abdulrahman

It is the *burning desire* that will get you out of bed. It is this *burning desire* that will occupy every spare moment you have. It will be the last thing you think of before going to sleep, and it will be the first thing you think of when you wake. If you have a goal, and you don't think about it with excitement, then your desire is not strong enough. The key is to have a strong reason for needing to achieve this goal and to ask yourself, exactly what the consequences of *not* achieving it are. Have a clear image in your mind of what it feels like to have achieved the goal. Picture it; smell it; taste it. Now that you have your goal in the forefront of your mind, ask yourself, "What do I need to do to get there?"

You must attach an emotional element to your end reward. If your end reward lacks an emotional connection, then your desire will not last the test of time. For example, if you start a business with the intention of earning one thousand dollars a week, unless you have an emotional connection, the chances are you will crumble. Yet if you had a target of hitting one thousand dollars a week because it would mean you can help your family with day-to-day living and remove their stress (if seeing them in stress really hurts you), then you will have a strong desire that will withstand the test of time. Your desire will only get stronger. People will feel your heat.

Break your goals down into small steps. A lot of people are scared of reaching higher ground, but it is amazing what heights you can achieve when you take one step at a time. Take one small step at a time and you will get to the top in the end.

GAME TIME

You have decided to play a new game. You want to become a professional gamer so you choose a game that is a lot more challenging. Your friends might mock and say that you are a fool for choosing such a hard game. Your friends might not want to be top gamers; they are content playing the easy games that feel and look good, but they never grow. That's their choice. Your *why* is different, and hence, you are pursuing what is important to you. Although you want to get to the end of the game, you don't know how you're going to do it. You simply play the game one level at a time.

"I dream for a living."
—Steven Spielberg, dreamer, director, producer, and screenwriter

All successful people are dreamers. Not to dream is not to live. Who wants to be a professional athlete?

Who wants to be a best-selling author? Who wants to retire early?

Who wants to travel the world? A few times over?

Who wants to party for a living, knowing their finances are in order?

Who wants to be a great parent, friend, or spouse? Who wants to live life on their own terms?

All successful people are dreamers. Bill Gates, the founder of Microsoft, was a dreamer. Sam Morgan, the founder of Trade Me, was a dreamer. Steve Jobs, the founder of Apple, was a dreamer. Pierre Omidyar, the founder of eBay, was a dreamer. Richard Branson, the founder of Virgin, was a dreamer. Steven Spielberg, the world renowned director/producer, was a dreamer. Michael Jordan, the basketball phenomenon, was a dreamer. P. Diddy, the name in entertainment, was a dreamer. There are thousands of dreamers, and many would have simply laughed at each of their dreams before they achieved them. Today they live their dreams. So can you.

"All successful people, men and women, are big dreamers. They imagine what their future could be, ideal in every respect, and then they work every day toward their distant vision, that goal or purpose."
—Brian Tracy, leading self-help author, coach, and motivational speaker)

Successful people make decisions based on their own beliefs, dreams, and reality. Your reality is not your friend's reality. Neither is right or wrong; we are simply all different. The determination, the drive, the dream—these are all unique to every individual. Whatever you can dream, you can have. I once heard that we only dream of things that are truly a possibility for us to achieve. There is a reason why you are able to dream of certain things while many can't dream that same dream for themselves. I firmly believe that we are able to achieve whatever we can visualize. Otherwise, we would never have been given the powerful ability to imagine.

But how would you know where to shoot if you didn't have a target? Would a runner ever start a marathon not knowing where the finish line was? Would you jump in your car without knowing which direction you were heading in? (Some of you might at times.) Is it a good idea to have a target? You bet every dollar it is.

If you want to have a new car, you must be specific as to what you want. You could say I want a nice home. What is a nice home? The answer would vary ten times if you asked ten different individuals. A nice home could be a waterfront apartment to one person and a house out of town on a block of land for someone else.

Here's a powerful tool for you to use:

I never used to believe in dream boards. A dream board is a piece of cardboard that contains pictures of all the things you want and be in your life. I personally used to think they were a waste of time—that was, until I saw a few successful friends have them all over their homes. And I decided to give them a go. I've always thought, successful people have what I want, so I'll do what they do. I can tell you that it's amazing to have personalized dream boards that you can look at on a daily basis. In fact, your dream board will do so much more if you can see it as often as possible in a day. I have friends who spend minutes on end staring at their dream boards. It seems to bring them a source of energy so they can go out there and have a productive day.

We all have days when we simply feel drained. We all have days when we are down. We are only human after all. As much as we like to think that we're creatures of logic, we're not. We're ruled by emotions, and it's draining.

Mobile phones have become a necessity in our day-to-day lives. What do you do to your phone when it runs low on battery? You recharge it. We are no different than mobile phones. We run out of battery life, and we need recharging. When we don't recharge our batteries, we run on empty. People run on empty for days, weeks, months, even years and wonder why they are not achieving at a top level in life. They wonder why their life is not where it's supposed to be. Simply looking at your dream board every day for a few minutes will be the charger for the battery of your strong desire.

"Successful people are dreamers who have found a dream too exciting, too important to remain in the realm of fantasy. Day by day, hour by hour, they toil in the service of their dream until they can see it with their eyes and touch it with their hands."
—Earl Nightingale, motivational speaker

Simple steps to having your personalized dream boards:

1. Get a few 40 X 30-centimeter cardboard sheets from a local stationary shop. You can even use A5 paper if you like. Use anything that you can stick a few nice photos on to admire.

2. Look at pictures in magazines that you like. Check out the magazines or Internet sites where you know you'll find images of the things you desire. You might want materialistic things like earrings, shoes, cars, or luxury hideaways. You might want a passionate relationship, for which you can find a picture depicting a happy couple. You might want to be an Olympic champion, and so you can find a picture of a gold medal and look at it every day.

3. Spend some time ensuring you have a dream board that is completely and utterly you. The dream board should be a snapshot of what your life is about to become. The images should stir up strong emotions in you. If they don't, keep looking for what you want. You will know when you find the right pictures for your dream board. They will always be something that brings a smile to your face, ear-to-ear.

What does your dream board say about you? Does it represent your dream life five years from now? Remember, there are no restrictions here. You are limited only by your own imagination. Are the dream boards a perfect snapshot of your dream life?

Who else, apart from yourself, will benefit once you achieve your dream?

_____

_____

A word of caution: You might be shocked to find that you may start having the things you want in your life as time goes by ... so be careful what you wish for, and with what you put on your dream board!

If anyone ever tells you to be realistic, choose to be *unrealistic*.

Your dreams may be unrealistic to them but a complete *reality* for you.

After all, what is reality?

What's my reality? What's your reality? What is your friend's reality?

Aren't they all so different?

So there is no reason why we should make other people's reality ours. We are born to live the dream we want. It is our right to live the life we desire. Not doing so is unjust.

Learn to expect to live your dream, for it should be your reality.

"The only reality I agree with is mine, not the reality of the majority."
—Kevin Abdulrahman

You must write your specific goals on paper if you want to win the game of life. People usually talk about their so-called goals but, unfortunately, are not committed to attaining them. Because those goals are not written, they just casually drift by.

Successful people write their specific dreams and goals into reality. Everyone I know who is successful has come to learn and understand the power of writing goals. I never used to write my goals. I used to think, "Hey, I don't need to write my goals down. I'm bright enough to keep them in my head.

"I'll remember it," I used to boast. Sure, I did remember my goals, but the question I have learned to ask is, "How often during the day am I thinking about my goals?" We are always so preoccupied with day-to-day chores that we don't get a chance to constantly think about our goals. What I found was that a month would go by, and I would get so preoccupied with the bills, the cat, the Internet connection, my friend's girlfriend problems, the gym, my car—you think about it, it was on my mind—that at the end of the month when I would get some breathing time, I'd look back and go, "*Wow*, that was one heck of a wasted month." I learned this truth the hard way when things were not coming to fruition. Women are usually better at multitasking, but most men can only do one thing at a time. We are already on the back foot when it comes to having goals in our minds. We all have things happening all the time, and since we can only attend to one thing at a time in our heads, the goal is straight out the door. This can drag on for weeks, months, and even years. Only after a while do we realize that we have deviated completely from our goals.

Most people are left wondering how the year went by so quickly. Successful people know that every day spent focusing on the end reward moves them one step closer to attaining their goals or living their dream lives.

Write ten goals, big or small, that you would like to achieve in the next twelve months. Write them down—write 'em, write 'em, write 'em.

_____

_____

_____

_____

_____

_____

_____

_____

You should make this list , not because Kevin is saying so but because, when you write down your goals, you have made a commitment, albeit to yourself. You have written something down and your subconscious is now telling you to go and make it happen. When you read your goals (to yourself; no one else has to hear them), you are taking your thoughts from your conscious mind to your subconscious mind. Put simply without getting clinical, the conscious mind controls such activities as kicking a ball. Your subconscious mind controls your breathing and your heartbeat.

Training your subconscious mind will help you to attain your dreams. Your subconscious mind never sleeps, so when you write your goal down and read it, you are putting your mind into training mode. Just imagine having a powerhouse working towards your goals twenty-four hours a day, seven days a week, the power of which you will only realize when you practice what I have written here.

Now when you have your goals written down and you've place them where they will be seen often throughout your day, you will be constantly reminded of what your priority in life is. You get to ask yourself the question and, right then and there, you can make the decision to keep on track. Constantly looking at your written goals is a path-correcting mechanism. Ants do it all the time; they use the sun as their navigation tool so as to get where they want to go. They move in figure eights and constantly use the sun and its angle as a guide to their destination. So, for lack of a better metaphor, be an *ant*.

I have heard that the difference between millionaires and billionaires is that millionaires read their goals once a day, and billionaires read theirs twice a day. I have heard this many times and, although I can't find any hard evidence of it, I sincerely believe it to be a true fundamental. Could it hold true with those who win the gold medal, and the people who come in fourth? I would suggest this to be the case. Your average Joe probably spends more time planning his vacation than planning his life and, hence, remains an average Joe.

To give you a personal example, I asked myself which part of my apartment I walked past most often. The spot happened to be around the pantry area because I love food. I took the list of goals that I wanted to achieve for the year and placed them in the most visited spot of the apartment—yes, the pantry. Now things didn't go to plan, as they often don't, but about halfway through the year, I noticed that I was spending more time at my laptop writing my books and less time visiting the pantry than I'd thought I would. I took the list and stuck it right next to my laptop. I achieved more in the next month than I had in the previous six months. Coincidence? I think not.

I see the list often enough every day that my brain can't distinguish fiction from fact. Having your dreams and goals in front of you all the time will transform what is fiction today into a reality tomorrow.

Never ever ever ever ever let go of your goals and dreams.

Take Home Message

Your goals and dreams are your reality. Let people feel your heat. Become *"burning hot."*

11

"It's simply a matter of doing what you do best and not worrying about what the other fellow is going to do"

– John R. Amos (fought in the American Civil War)

BUYING IT VERSUS LEAVING IT

It is said that the cheapest commodity in this world is people's opinion because everyone has a truckload to give away. The sad part that fuels this phenomenon is that it's free, and, unfortunately, most of it is worth its weight in rubbish. Every Tom, Dick, and Harriet has something to say. You can't stop people from giving opinions, but you sure can choose how to deal with them.

Here's the bottom line. You are in control. You choose whether to accept those opinions or not. You choose whether you let what Tom says affect you, and you choose whether Dick's criticisms makes you feel down and out. You choose whether what Harriet thinks of you affects how you do your business.

Always consider this—if those people giving you their opinions don't have what you want or aren't where you want to be, then why should you accept their opinions? Just think about it. Why take their opinion if that's all they are giving away? Someone might think that it's a good idea for you to jump off a cliff, but would you do it? Someone else might think that it's a good idea for your child to hang around street gangs, but would you agree to it? One person might think that your spouse isn't the right person for you, but would you swap? (Some of you might.) Another might not like the shirt you're wearing, but would you let others choose your clothes for you? Isn't it interesting that most poor people like to give their advice on how to make money and become rich? Isn't it interesting that most people will tell you how to have a successful relationship when they're going through their eleventh spouse?

I have always asked myself—and, at times, challenged some friends who wanted to give me their opinions to answer—this question: I would say something like this, "I like to have a lavish life so I will need a fair amount of money to keep me happy. Being the spontaneous person that I am, I could be in New York one day and feel like sitting on the beautiful sands in the Gold Coast of Australia the next. I could be walking on the Great Wall of China midweek and then want to head to Pisa to admire the leaning tower for the weekend. I want to be able to give my family whatever they need, without a blink. That would cost a lot purely in monetary terms. You are suggesting very strongly that I do not do this project, so would you be able to wire the funds that I require into my account every year?"

To this, every friend would stutter and then always (can't seem to find one that will take the bait) say, "*No.*"

I would turn around and say, "So if you can't give me what I want, would you be kind enough not to give me your opinions either? I am an all or nothing guy; how about you give me *all* or nothing." I never hear their opinion from that point on. It's a bit harsh, but it helped me stay focused.

Imagine shopping for groceries at your local supermarket. You want some fruit, vegetables, milk, orange juice, and some pasta for dinner. You enter armed with your list, knowing exactly what you need to buy. But is what you want all that there is on offer in the supermarket?

Oh no. Supermarkets are great at strategically displaying thousands of products, all to tempt you to pick them up off the shelves. Let me ask you, how many times have you fallen for this marketing ploy? How many times have you ended up buying things that were not on your shopping list, things that you had no intention of buying? Those products did not just jump off the shelf and into your basket (although at times it feels like it). Those who are on a strict budget and those who are serious about going in and getting out are usually the best at avoiding this trap. They simply go in, buy what they come for, and leave—*mission accomplished.*

Your life is like going through a supermarket. It's filled with people's opinions. It's completely up to you what ends up in your basket, which will determine what you take through the checkout with you. Successful people have mastered the art of being able to keep opinions shelved with the owner. They have acquired and mastered the eleventh SECRET WEAPON, *listening only to the right person in the right field.* Just because someone has an opinion doesn't mean you have to buy it. Successful people are good at becoming unaffected by opinions, good or bad. They go with what they have set out to do. They go with their shopping list.

Again, we don't let others choose the clothes we wear. We don't let others choose our spouse, the sport we play, or our friends. Therefore, never let someone else choose how you should live your life. You are not disrespecting anyone; you're just choosing not to take in the opinions others are offering—it's that *simple.*

"Too bad that all the people who know how to run the country are busy driving taxicabs and cutting hair."
—George Burns, Academy Award-winning Jewish American comedian, actor, and writer

Fear and personal limitations rule most people's realities. People give you their opinions based on their own fears. They will talk you out of an idea or a venture you might be planning. Unfortunately, these people are often those who are the closest to you. They don't really want to do you harm, but in most instances, they have absolutely no clue what they are talking about. If they did, they would be doing something about it rather than giving their opinion.

GAME TIME

A friend arrives whilst you are playing the game. You are at an early stage in the game and are moving ahead enthusiastically. Unexpectedly, your friend starts to ridicule you for playing this game. He or she might ridicule you for not being able to go through the levels quickly enough or tell you that the game is just not for you. This person may even tell you why you shouldn't play the game at all. Or conversely, your friend might tell you how you should play the game, even though he or she hasn't ever played this particular game before. This friend might be sure that other games are better suited to you. Your friend has told you *a whole lot of garbage. As a true gamer, proving these people wrong is rather satisfying. You have picked your game; it's time you straightened out some opinions with your results.*

"I agree with no one's opinion. I have some of my own."
—Ivan Turgenev, Russian author and poet

We can't help how many opinions are made available to us, especially in this day and age. When each person seems to want to offload a dozen opinions at a time, we have the choice to buy into their opinions or let them slip away at the same speed that they came toward us.

Practice picturing an imaginary shield between you and those who are opinionated. Every time someone generously shares with you their unwanted opinions, you can put up this imaginary shield and in your mind simply throw it back to them. It's a very simple process. Just keep smiling and walk away, continuing to do what's right for you. The people offering the opinions won't even realize that you are not taking it on board. Another technique is one I call "the *mute button*." Imagine yourself holding a remote control and, when someone starts to voice an unwanted opinion, simply make a gesture with your thumb (as if you are pressing the mute button on a TV remote). The opinion giver doesn't have to see you do it, but it's a personal reminder for yourself to let it slide. I have found both techniques very effective in my journey to success. Try it! You'll have a lot of fun.

I always use the following example in my talks about opinions, and it's about my dear mother. I love my mother, and I have an immense amount of respect for her. But when one day my beautiful S55 AMG Mercedes super car decided to not start anymore, no amount of love and respect for my mother would get my car fixed. It didn't matter how much she thought she knew about cars or how many opinions she had about what had gone wrong; she still wouldn't have been able to fix it. I had to take the S55 to a mechanic. The car required an expert to get it fixed, not just anyone (or everyone) with an opinion.

The same applies when you have a sore tooth and it needs to be pulled out. Would you go to your mechanic for that? Or maybe a best friend? Would you take the opinion of your plumber on how to handle it? Without any disrespect to these professionals or friends, you need a good dentist who has the knowledge and skills to do the job properly.

You will never be liked by everyone when you are heading to the top of your game. This is the reality all successful people face. In whatever field you're playing your game, there's always a myriad of ill-willed chitchatting, backstabbing, and put-downs that will match your level of success. Those few who are winning the game make no time to listen to other people's opinions. They make no time to justify what they're doing. As long as you know, in your heart, that you're doing the right thing, then pursue your passion and let your results speak for themselves. Never let anyone else dictate what you should do and how you should do it, unless they have done what you want to do and have what you want to have. They usually don't.

By proving that you can produce results, you'll be able to reduce, though you can never eliminate, the opinions people give to you and about you.

As a result,of weeding out opinions of those who aren't in the know, successful people surround themselves with people who are better than themselves in their field of choice. They partner up with the experts. So always look for people who have what you want, whether it's a passionate relationship, great friendships, top work ethics, or a successful business, and listen to their suggestions. Remember when your parents told you to stay away from "the bad kids," in the fear that you might be influenced by them. They were right. The same also applies to winning the game of life. Surround yourself with successful people, and you can't help but be influenced by them. This will help propel you to win your game of life. Successful people go with their gut feelings and are smart enough to only listen to the right people in the right field. Respect *everyone*, but listen only to people who are experts in their own field (whatever that is). These experts have earned the right to voice an opinion, but even then, it's only an opinion.

A very wealthy gentleman once told me a story that helped me immensely through my journey of success. I later found out it could have been his version of an old Aesop's fable. Nonetheless, the moral of the story helped me immensely throughout my journey.

This is the story the gentleman told me:

There once was an Italian farmer who decided to take a day trip to his local village with his wife, child, and his trusted donkey. It was a nice day and the sun was shining. The farmer jumped on the donkey and had his wife and child walk alongside him. As he entered the city, he could see people on both sides looking at them strangely and whispering. He overheard one say, "Look what this world has come to; this man is comfortable on the donkey while the poor wife is walking in this heat." So the farmer decided to have the wife hop on the donkey too in the hope that this would stop the whispering. They continued on, and a few hundred meters down the track, he saw another group of people staring at them strangely and whispering. He overheard one say, "Look what this world has come to; this couple is enjoying a comfortable ride while they are making this poor child walk in the heat."

The farmer got upset and decided that he and his wife should get off the donkey. He then placed his child on the donkey, and the family carried on their journey, the farmer walking alongside the donkey with his wife. Only a hundred meters on, the farmer could see people now talking loudly about his family. They were saying, "Look what this world has come to; this young child is sitting comfortably on the donkey whilst his older parents are walking in the heat. How shameful."

In frustration, the farmer asked the child to come down, grabbed the donkey and placed it on his shoulders, and started walking, along with his wife and child. Now people were laughing very hard. He could hear people yelling now saying,

"Look at what this world has come to. A donkey is supposed to serve its master, and now the master seems to be giving the donkey a comfortable ride."

The farmer snapped. "That's it," he said. This is my wife, my child, and my donkey, and I will do as I please. He put the donkey down, jumped on it, and proceeded on his journey as he'd started, with his wife and child walking alongside.

The moral of the story: No matter what you do, people will talk, and they'll give you opinions. Do what you know in your heart is best and mind your own business. You'll exhaust yourself trying to impress and please everyone.

Also remember, when the tables are turned, to ensure that you're giving an informed point of view (when asked for it) rather than an opinion you might have. Do yourself a favor—always put your opinion aside and look at the information in your hands. Never prejudge people or information you might be given based on what you think you already know.

Have you been buying more opinions than you should have up until now? (*Be honest.*)

_____

_____

Using what you have read, what two steps *must* you take toward deciding whether you are buying an opinion or leaving it?

_____

_____

Take Home Message

In the end, you are in control. You choose to buy it or leave it.

12

THE SHINING ARMOR

What do most people like? Who are most people attracted to? What do most people look for in a person? What type of person would most people bank on?

If you were to choose a person (for whatever reason), would you choose the one who is shy or insecure or the other who is confident?

Would you pick a person who sings and smiles? Or would you ta ke someone who is, like the majority, seemingly about to break down and cry or start up a fight? In this chapter, I'm going to start off dealing with the surface aspect; then I'll peel back to the center of it, like an onion. People say, "Don't judge a book by its cover." But guess what, people do. Whether you like it or not, people will judge you the first time they see you. Whether you like it or not, people will make an instant judgment on whom they think you are.

How are you coming across on your first impression? Are you leaving a lasting first impression where people look forward to seeing you again? Are you getting what you want when you meet with a prospect in business? Are you leaving people with a positive vibe?

If you aren't getting the desired result in any situation, you must change your method. Some say that first impressions don't count. Those who say this are usually the same people who aren't good at making first impressions. Remember to choose who you listen to. Every successful person will tell you that first impressions do count because they are the bases on which you build your profile. Do people look at you and think "Whatever this person has, I want it"? Or do they say, "Whatever this person has, I don't want it"? You always want to make sure people fall in the first category.

So what underlies a good first impression?

Successful people have it and those who don't, envy it. Those lacking this key ingredient think it's arrogance, but they're mistaken. Successful people make great first impressions because they ooze confidence in whatever they set their minds to. They are confident compared to the majority of people, who lack self esteem. Take me to a room, and I will be able to spot the successful individuals purely from their air of confidence. You can usually see it in their posture. You can feel their vibrations.

They have a *presence*.

Most people usually focus on the content of what they have to say. Whatever you have to say means nothing if you don't put confidence behind it. What you have to say could be of great value; yet with no confidence, you will lose your audience. Have you heard people complain that they can't seem to get others to listen to them? They get pushed around when talking about a business opportunity, or they're not taken seriously by family and friends. No one will want to sign them up to their music label, no one will go out on a date with them, no one will join them on a business venture, no one will sponsor them in their sport, and no one will buy from them if they don't exude confidence. You don't usually hear confident people complaining of the same concerns.

Think of confidence as a shining armor. Without it, you're vulnerable. With it, you're protected, attractive, and magnetic. As you wear your shining armor, you'll attract others to you. In this world, people are after the very few who will stand and give their message with confidence. People are after guarantees in life.

Unfortunately, there is no such thing, so the closer you can be to a guarantee, the more people will listen. If you are confident, without a shadow of doubt, in whatever it is you want to achieve and be, the world is yours. Nobody can get through your shining armor.

To lack confidence is to lack your shining armor.

There is a fine line between being confident and being arrogant. Ensure that you are confident, but never become arrogant. Arrogance falls under what we discussed earlier—being a know-it-all. Confidence is to believe in yourself and in what you do. Remember that other people's opinions mean nothing because, no matter what you do, there will always be people who, due to their low self-esteem, fear, and limitations, will see your confidence as arrogance.

Confidence is something you must develop in whatever you wish to do.

Notice I did not say, "Be confident." We all start from the same point. We may lack confidence in different aspects of our lives, but there is no reason why we can't develop it. Develop a vision and immense belief in whatever you do and make it clear to everyone around you that you are focused on your goal. You will not be swayed by other people's worthless opinions. Let your actions speak and show that you've made up your mind about to live your dream and you're going to see it through to the end. When you have the focus, the vision, and the belief, you will appear confident, and you will be confident.

If you're uncertain about yourself, what you do, or the product you're selling, how can you expect others to listen to you? How can you expect to win your game?

To develop confidence, you must look at the beliefs you hold. Successful people have developed the twelfth SECRET WEAPON: having *positive, unshakeable beliefs* that help them to be confident in whatever they put their minds into. Old, destructive beliefs can be changed. A belief is merely a point of view that we can change by making a decision. Beliefs can be changed in a heartbeat. You become aware of your beliefs and simply make a snap decision as to whether those beliefs are serving you well or whether they're not. You are where you are today because of the beliefs you have in life. To become confident, you must develop *positive, unshakeable beliefs*. Only then will you obtain the results you desire. You can't believe that you'll never be rich and expect to become rich. You can't believe that you'll never be an Olympic athlete and become an Olympic athlete. You can't believe that you can't find your soul mate and then expect to find your soul mate.

Your belief must be aligned with what you want. If you truly believe you'll become rich, be a top athlete, or meet your soul mate, then things will start happening for you in your life. So start believing the right thoughts and work toward obtaining them. This will take time, so don't expect to get the results in an hour. You must consciously practice having *positive, unshakeable beliefs* for a period of time. At first this will feel a bit scary, but as you continue to practice what you do, you'll become more and more confident. Just remember that, if someone has done it before you, you can do it too. They're no different and no better than you. And even if no one has done it before, remember that someone has to be first.

GAME TIME

When you're playing a game, you must believe that you can, and will get through the level. Otherwise, you'll give up because you won't see a light at the end of the tunnel. If you believe that you can't do it, the result will be that you'll stop trying. Yet others know that, despite challenges, they'll be able to get through. Never stop believing, for believing is what will help you keep going. Have faith in the positive. Especially, always remember that if someone else has done it, you can too.

"Your external confidence represents your internal belief."
—Kevin Abdulrahman

List three beliefs you currently have about yourself .

_____

_____

_____

Are these beliefs aligned with the result you want to achieve? In other words, do you think people who have achieved what you want to achieve have these beliefs?

Yes ☐   No ☐

Where do those beliefs come from?

_____

_____

_____

What three *positive, unshakeable beliefs* do you need so you can have the confidence you need in order to win the game of your life?

_____

_____

_____

What do you think you need to do to get these *positive, unshakeable beliefs*?

_____

_____

_____

How quickly can your old beliefs be changed to the new ones?

_____

Hint: *A heartbeat*

Here's a suggestion: Most people's lack of belief or negative belief is a result of what they don't know. One way to create positive beliefs and to build on having unshakeable beliefs is to investigate and really learn about whatever it is you're focusing on. I remember coaching a client who I knew was destined to become great. He seemed stuck in the business venture he was in and was simply not getting the results he wanted. I shared with him something that someone once shared with me.

I refer to it as "The Table."

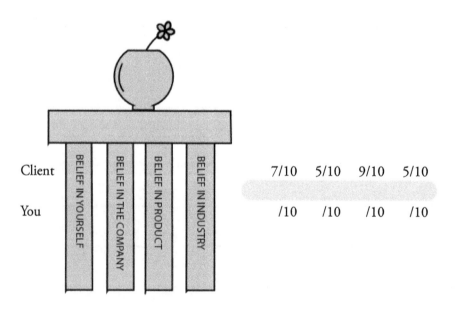

Fig. 1
The Table

Note: these four categories applied to a client of mine. You may change the categories to the four main belief areas that apply (institution, entity, or situation, for example), but the essence remains the same.

I asked my client to rank his belief level in each category on a scale of 1 – 10. I told him that there wasn't a right or wrong answer. It was important for him to answer each honestly, and he did. His numbers were as shown in the diagram.

"Change your beliefs, and you will change your life."
—Kevin Abdulrahman

If his current numbers were indicative of the size of each table leg, then the table wouldn't be very stable. I then pointed out that he needed to study more about his company and also the industry he was working in. I told him not to use this exercise in realizing his lack of belief as a scapegoat but rather as a tool to propel him to having unshakeable beliefs. I also said that if, after his research he finds that his beliefs are still low, then he must look at an alternative project in which he can truly get his belief levels up. Fast forward a year and when I last heard of him, my client was in the top earning bracket in the same company in his region. Obviously, he'd educated himself more about his company and the industry he was working in and built his belief to a point where doing well in his business became a natural process.

What can you count on?

You can count on people telling you these things:

"You *can't* do that."

"That *doesn't* work."

"Don't most people *fail* trying this?"

"This will *never* work."

"You're dreaming; that will never happen."

People who say these things are fearful people. They have no courage, and they're trying to share their *fear* with you. You will not be the only lucky one to experience this. Everyone does. What separates successful people from the majority is the shining armor they wear to deflect the negative opinions. Don't have a bar of it. There is nothing sweeter than making a point by achieving what you said you would do. Some people get caught up wasting their energy trying to defend themselves. Remember, you only have so much energy. Put your energy toward your dream, and you will achieve your dream. As you start taking positive steps toward your goal, you will develop *positive, unshakeable beliefs*, and your armor will grow thicker and glow brighter. Your confidence will grow to new heights, and your presence will be, well …

magnetic.

 Name an area in your life where you have the least confidence. (*Be honest.*)

_____

_____

What two things could you do to build confidence in that area, in order for you to win your game of life?

_____

_____

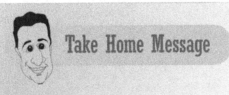

You must wear your
shining armor if you want to
succeed.

13

"*If you want to be successful, find someone who has achieved the results you want and copy what they do and you'll achieve the same results*"

-*Anthony Robbins (a top authority on peak performance)*

THE FAST TRACK

Some people see what someone has—the quality of the person's friendships and other relationships, his or her business success, the way the person lead his or her life, and they decide to directly/indirectly model that person. That's a smart move. After all, why spend all your energy creating a new path when someone else has potentially done all the hard work? All you have to do is follow a proven path. Why reinvent the wheel, so to speak, when you can simply spend your energy getting further ahead on that working wheel?

Always remember that there is nothing special about that person who is doing well in life. You may have an idol, or you may even have hundreds of idols. You may have an inspiring mentor figure. You may know people who are examples of what you want and others who are examples of what you don't want in your life. They may be good-looking, and they may be good at what they do, but I assure you that every one of them started just the same. I am the first to admit that some will have special attributes that seem to help them in certain aspects of life. In general, though, everyone has some form of uniqueness and ability that allows him or her to do whatever he or she set his or her mind to.

The person who is doing well in life now is not necessarily better than you. He or she just knows something and is working with that knowledge. Success always leaves a trail, and if you look hard enough you'll find it. By then, like many, you'll have already solved half the equation. Many times you don't have to look too hard; the answer comes knocking on your door. You simply need to open the door. That's the first half of the equation, and it's simple. The second half is simple as well. I'm not saying easy because easy implies that it can be obtained without much effort, and that's not true.

Some people become stuck in the second half of the equation. They find the path to their goldmine. However, ego kicks in, and many decide to reinvent the wheel. They feel that they can do something better, make it more glitzy, add their genius ideas, extra functions, and more. They end up going down a different path than the people they want to model followed and, hence, get different results. They never see what they have done, often wondering why things aren't working out for them. Sadly, as a result, some stop a few meters short of their goldmine.

Become good at duplicating those who have won their game of life. In most instances, you don't have to reinvent the wheel. The wheel is already there. Just get it moving in the same direction and in the same way as the successful person before you, and it will lead you to win your game too. If someone is making ten thousand dollars a week passively, you can find out what it is they did and how long it took , what they had to do, and what sacrifices they made to get there. You choose whether you want to model that or not. If you do, then model what they did to get what they have. Pick any aspect of life you want to succeed in. Pick out your mentors and work on modeling them. Successful people have learned the thirteenth SECRET WEAPON: being *master duplicators*. They really capture the essence of what made someone win his or her game of life, and they duplicate it to a tee. This could mean they've had personal, face-to-face access to the successful individual they're emulating, but that's not necessarily the case. I know many successful individuals who have modeled other successful people through listening to their CDs, reading their books, and attending seminars and webinars.

I want to share with you something not usually mentioned in discussions of success.

A lot of people actually fail in modeling the results they are aiming to achieve.

Why?

If everyone says that the fastest way to winning the game of your life is to model someone who has already succeeded, then why do many still fail?

Has this possibly happened to you or to someone you know?

You may have started a business because you have seen others do well in that particular business, yet you may not have achieved the desired result. You could have taken up a sport and yet didn't get to the level you were hoping for, even though you were modeling successful people who were doing the same. They were getting the results. You modeled them, and still, you failed.

Herein lies the problem. Chances are you thought you were modeling the successful person, but you didn't. You weren't a *master duplicator*. Many see these successful people and start copying what they're doing today. Chances are, they're in the enjoyment phase (see graph in fig. 2) of their lives. They are harvesting their fruits, eating them slowly, and savoring every moment. If you walk in and decide to copy their behavior starting *today*, you'll not get what they have. You must do as they did when they were in the initial stages; in other words, if it's business success that the person you're hoping to emulate has, the chances are that he or she worked twenty-nine hours a day, ten days a week to make it to where he or she is today. You must do the same. You must model the successful person each step of the way, starting from the beginning.

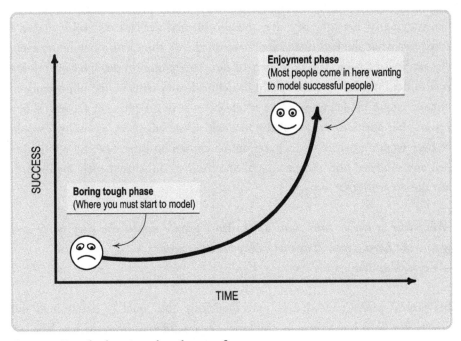

Fig. 2—Graph showing the phases of success

I'll give you a real life example. With one of my business ventures a long time ago, my partners and I had promoted having fun whilst doing the business. We were a young, vibrant, and outgoing group of individuals. I suggested that we work hard and then play hard. So the idea was to work the business and, after putting in effective, income-producing hours during the week, we would play soccer and go out socialising in the weekend as a group. A funny thing began to happen. All the guys who were just starting the business modeled the guys already successful in the business. They would be at the soccer games, at the BBQs, and at the clubs, yet they weren't performing well in their business. They got the fun part (because it was the easiest to do), but they forgot to do what these successful people had to do before they got to the stage of enjoying themselves—work through the boring, tough phase.

These days, I spend most of my time in cafés, reading the paper and keeping up to date with current affairs. I also spend a lot of time catching up with friends. I remember when a young lady asked if she could have what I have. I said sure, if that's what you want. I told her that she needed to do what successful people did to have what successful people have. Six months went by, and I got a call from her. She was rather unhappy and told me that things didn't work out for her. Judging by her tone of voice, she also blamed her lack of results on me. I asked her what she had done. She mentioned that she spent a few hours every day reading the paper and doing what I did. Yet six months on, she wasn't doing well in her business. I couldn't help but chuckle and reiterate the importance of understanding modeling based on where she was in the phase of success. When I was in her position, to have a latte in a café would have been a novelty. I would be busy working twenty hours a day on my chosen business. She chose to ignore that and modeled only the easy parts. She chose to do what she felt she liked. It just doesn't work that way.

"Modeling is easier said than done. Most people model the easy parts and ignore the hard parts. That's why they lack the results."
—Kevin Abdulrahman

Be wary of whom and what you are modeling. You could be determined and driven, but don't jump the gun, thinking you are different from the rest. The law of gravity applies to us all. Every dream requires the right effort over a period of time to obtain the result you desire. Always remember the graph when modeling someone you aspire to be like. You can probably go through the graph a lot faster than the person you are modeling, but you still have to go through it. Modeling takes time.

Consider this: I want to model a friend of mine who has a great physique. In order to do so, I must lose ten kilograms of fat and gain five kilograms of muscle. I will need to start a very strict nutrition plan as of today and hit the gym for an initial workout of an hour a day, five days a week. I will need to incorporate a lot of cardio into my routine.

Can I come out of the gym after my second session expecting to have the physique of my friend? Can I do what he is doing today in his enjoyment phase, expecting to get his result?

Absolutely not. I must go through the graph. I must go through the boring and tough phase. I must work on being a *master duplicator.*

No one in his or her right mind will expect to come out with the desired result overnight. We would like to, but we know that results take time. Modeling also requires you to do exactly the same things as the person you're modeling. You cannot add your own variation to things and expect the same result. If my friend is on a strict nutrition plan, takes top-quality supplements, and does a high-intensity workout, I can't expect the same results if I consume low-quality supplements, do a low-intensity workout, and eat a diet of burgers and fries. Sure I am modeling on face value, so to speak, but that is not true modeling. Most people are not honest about this matter. They say that they're modeling, but they're only doing so on the surface. That doesn't work.

Name an instant when you thought you modeled and yet didn't achieve the desired result? (*Be honest.*)

_____

_____

Name two people whom you admire in life.

_____

_____

What two things must you do to fast-track your results?

_____

_____

Take Home Message

The only way to fast track
your game of life is to
model the tough phase

14

"*Being busy and being productive
are not necessarily related*"

-Brian Koslow(author and entrepreneur)

DOING THE BUSINESS

You've woken up in the morning and made breakfast for yourself and your family; you've taken the kids to school before heading to work. During your lunchtime, you manage to grab a bite whilst paying the bills because they're piling up, and you don't want to pay the late penalty fee. You finish work, and you come home. You grab a cup of tea, and you take the kids to their sports game. Once that's done, you bring them home so they can get their homework done whilst you prepare dinner. You've got the laundry to do in the meantime and, since you're a multitasker, you return your best friend's call for a chat to see how his or her day is going. It's time for dinner, which you enjoy as a family, followed by preparing to send the kids to bed. You have the privilege of bringing your work home, and you go through some files over a cup of hot chocolate. Pretty soon, you feel your eyelids getting heavy, and you fall asleep. The cycle repeats the next day. Days go by, weeks go by and, before you know it, it's another month. Then it's another year. Soon, a whole lifetime has just gone by …

And you've been existing every day, just being busy.

Successful people and unsuccessful people have the same twenty-four hours in a day. Today, most people have equal opportunities to access and use resources. Why is it that most people seem to run around frustrated without achieving much, whilst others seem to fit in so much with ease? When most people are running around like headless chickens, successful people have acquired and mastered the fourteenth SECRET WEAPON: being *productive*—not being busy, but *productive*. They are "doing the business." You must become aware of the difference between the two. Being *productive* means spending and in fact investing hours every day working towards any chosen task or goal until you bring it to completion. Being productive means doing what it is truly needed to get from A to B. Being *productive* means you are *doing the business*. Learn to spend some more productive hours throughout your day.

Now you may relate to the story at the beginning of this chapter, and if you don't, chances are you do know people who fit this scenario. Their stories may be different, but their situations are the same. Their lives always seem to be busy, yet they aren't achieving what they want. Why? Because they aren't being *productive* in the sense of achieving what they want in life

So let me come back to *you* for a second.

What are you doing?

Whenever anyone asks, "How are you doing?" what's the very first thought that comes into your head? Most people's immediate thought is, "I'm busy.". When you ask them a question, they tell you how busy they are; you see them stressing a lot because they don't seem to have enough hours in a day, and so they rightfully say, "I am so busy." But why is it that, with all the hours, people spend being busy, they don't achieve much success in life? They are simply leading busy lives.

Does this scenario sound familiar?

"Don't tell me how hard you work. Tell me how much you get done."
—James Ling, businessman who collected companies like they were baseball cards

Most people keep telling themselves, "I am so busy; I am so busy." But I always think to myself, "What are you busy doing?"

People have busy lives. It only seems like they're getting busier.

Many people are faced with the same circumstances and yet live a much fuller life. They are able to achieve higher grounds, business success, fruitful relationships, and so many of the other dreams and desires we all share. After all, don't we all have the same twenty-four hours in our day?

The difference: Unsuccessful people are busy being busy. Successful people are busy being productive.

Which of the two are you?

Here is a way you can get your own honest answer. The questions you must ask yourself *right now* are:

"Am I achieving much? Am I getting the results *I want* in life? Am I being productive?"

Most people confuse the concept of being busy with being productive.

One of them simply consumes your time with no result; the other helps you win the game of life and achieve massive success. Although I may not know you as an individual, and I may not have sat down with you to chat in depth about you and your personal circumstances, but I can say with great certainty that you spend less than ten productive hours a week. By productive hours, I mean hours that directly affect growth in whatever area you wish to focus on. Only 1 percent of people can say they put in ten or more productive hours a week. The rest spend their time being busy.

That's a bold statement; after all, I don't even know you. Let's find out, shall we? I have printed for you a schedule for Monday to Sunday. Now you can photocopy this if you want to and post it somewhere so that you constantly see it and are reminded of what you need to do.

Here is what you need to do:

Don't assume the hours for the coming week; let's work with what you've done last week, since that can't be changed and is proof to help you make a serious decision. Start with Monday, and go right through to Sunday. Note the hour slots (7:00 – 8:00 a.m., 8:00 – 9:00 a.m., 9:00 – 10:00 a.m., and so on, until 10:00 p.m.,).

	MONDAY	TUESDAY	WEDNESDAY	THURSDAY	FRIDAY	SATURDAY	SUNDAY
7am - 8am							
8am - 9am							
9am - 10am							
10am - 11am							
11am - 12pm							
12pm - 1pm							
1pm - 2pm							
2pm - 3pm							
3pm - 4pm							
4pm - 5pm							
5pm - 6pm							
6pm - 7pm							
7pm - 8pm							
9pm - 10pm							

Fig. 3
A productivity calendar

Think very hard about what you've done throughout the week and fill in the slots. Aim to fill in as much as possible, including coffee breaks, lunches, and the like. We are aiming to see how your week has gone by. Be as precise as you can.

Now this is where the exercise becomes interesting. Highlight with complete honesty the productive hours you have put in throughout your whole week, starting with Monday. Remember these are hours that result in you growing in life. You can highlight productive hours for your job, business, relationships, sports or what ever is of importance to you at this moment and time (photocopy this table and do a separate one for each area of focus).

How many hours were *productive*?

_____ hours

Over the last few years, I have been rather slack in going to the gym, and my eating habits have not been the best. As a result, I lost a lot of muscle mass and also gained some body fat, which I wanted to lose. A personal trainer friend of mine gave me a worksheet to monitor what goes into my body. I initially wondered why he did that, but he said that it would help me have an idea of what and how much I was eating. It was similar to the sheet I have printed here for you. I was asked to fill in what I was consuming every day and at what times. Then I would stare at the sheet at the end of a week to see what it looked like.

It was disastrous, to say the least. But I came to a point of self-realization. I am hoping you have come to that point with the exercise you just did.

That worksheet made me be aware all the stuff I happened to be putting into my body without realizing I was doing so. No wonder I was getting fat. I didn't even realize how bad my eating patterns had become and how much unhealthy food I was consuming. That process made me aware of what I needed to and needed not to eat. My intention was to lose some weight; yet I was consuming a lot of excess calories and remaining unaware that I ate so much and so badly. By monitoring and reducing my intake, I could then achieve my desired results—burning off those calories and losing fat.

Bringing the above example to life, work, business, sports or relationships, you are probably keeping busy, but chances are, you are not being productive. You may feel the world on your shoulders—putting in forty, sixty, eighty hours a week, yet your productive hours are probably under ten, with a push and a shove.

"The least productive people are usually the ones who are most in favor of holding meetings."
—Thomas Sowell, author and economist

Productive hours do not include those spent fluffing, filing, cleaning the desk, reorganizing clients lists, color-coding everything, constantly holding meetings, and doing other such busywork. Productive activities include making those business calls; spending quality time with the ones you love, enhancing your sports skills, training up by using the best systems; building the business, sales generation, attending self improvement classes—in other words,, whatever will help you rocket forward or become better at whatever it is you're focusing on.

Plan and focus on achieving more productive hours and watch your life flourish.

Five simple ways to double your productivity:

1.Prioritize your activities by planning your days, weeks, and months in advance. Planning for tomorrow will be much easier than planning for months to come. The more you can plan in advance though, the easier it will be to make decisions on what you can and can't do. You must learn and practice to plan your day in advance. This is a simple and powerful technique- plan for tomorrow today.

2. Itemize the tasks you need to do and prioritize them, one being the most important right through to, say, seven. Have a list of the seven things you must do. You are not to do number three until you do numbers one and two. You will find yourself achieving so much more with this technique.

Learn to quickly ascertain whether something is a productive activity or not. List it from one to seven. Focus on every individual task without trying to do fifteen things at once. Forget about trying to multi-task. One task at a time seems boring, but you will end up achieving more. The desired result is to at least double your productivity. That's a minimum.

Let's practice right now.

Write down seven things you need to do tomorrow. Itemize them from one to seven.

1.————————————————————————————

2. ————————————————————————————

3. ————————————————————————————

4. ————————————————————————————

5. _____

6. _____

7. _____

You cannot do number seven until you've done numbers five and six.

This technique is designed to force you to do the things you would otherwise put off till later. Do this on a daily basis; follow this principle, and I guarantee you will at least double your productivity.

3. Learn to say *no*. Most people say yes to everything. You might be working on a project when a friend invites you to a game of your favorite sport or to watch a movie you have been longing to see. As tempting as the offer is, you must learn to say no. At one point, my younger brother, Rami (keep an eye out for him at www.ramiabdulrahman.com), realized how ineffective he was in growing toward his success. He realized that he was driving around trying to help everyone who wanted a hand, and it was draining all his energy. I told him that he needed to stop and take time to fill his own cup. He said that doing so would be selfish. I suggested that he look at the other side of the coin. If his cup was full, he could give a lot more than when his cup was empty.

4. Focus on completing the task at hand. Distractions will be thrown at you left, right, and center. Let's say you wanted to start a fire using a magnifying glass; your goal would be impossible if you were constantly moving the lens. You can start a massive fire by holding on and focusing on one point for a period of time. Once you have established a fire, you can then move on to starting other fires. In the quest to grow and win the game, many make the mistake of being distracted with every second thing that comes their way. *Focus.* You must live a life where you develop extreme and immense focus.

People that are distracted by everything happening in their surroundings do not excel because they are so caught up in insignificant events. They spend their time and energy chasing ghosts. Since crises do occur, the key is to simply deal with them and then go back to your point of focus. It doesn't mean that you deny the fact that things happen and; oh yes, more often than not, they do. Just remember the magnifying glass. Focus and don't let anyone move your magnifying glass.

5. Make it a habit to be conscious of staying productive. Create a circle of like-minded friends and make it a rule to ask one another, "How has your day been?"

Every time anyone responds by saying, "I'm busy," they're fined five dollars. This can go into a kitty, which you could use at the end of the month toward purchasing more personal development CDs or books. It will take you out of the habit of saying, "I've been busy" and serve as a constant reminder of *how* you are spending your day.

 What two habits are eating up your valuable time? (*Be honest.*)

_____

_____

What two things *must* you do to help you be more productive in order to win your game of life?

_____

_____

Take Home Message

Always ask, "Is this productive? Am I 'doing the business'?"

15

"I lost today waiting for tomorrow"

– Kevin Abdulrahman

LATER SYNDROME

I should tidy up my office. Ah, I'll do it later.

I should really get myself a second stream of income to fund my hobby.

Ah, I'll do it later.

I must get around to writing my book. Ah, I'll do it later.

I should spend more time with my kids before they grow up.

Ah, I'll do it later.

I should really apply THE SECRET WEAPONS Kevin is sharing with me in *The Book*.

Ah, I'll do it later.

I should really spend an hour a day reading books that will help me get to my destination a lot more quickly.

Later.

Later, later, later.

"How soon 'not now' becomes never."
—Martin Luther, humorist, writer, and lecturer

I was stru ck with this syndrome for years. I make a decision everyday to combat it. The majority of people today have unfortunately been affected by this very nasty and contagious disease called *Later Syndrome*. This syndrome is deadly and also goes by the name familiar to most of us—procrastination. Stay away from it, like you would the plague. You will either conquer it by actively making a decision or allow it to consume you. Like always, the choice is yours.

Procrastination is when you must do something and you are simply not doing it. As I'm typing this, I can't help but wonder why we are all so guilty of doing such a silly thing. Procrastination used to be my best friend. I had so many brilliant thoughts and ways of doing whatever I was doing to make it big, but that's all they were for a long time, just thoughts.

Then one day I woke up. I woke up to realize I didn't want to be one of those many people who end up taking their best *billion*-dollar ideas to the grave with them. What good is your idea once you're gone? I realized how much I was missing out on. What I knew could make me millions. Others were doing it, whilst I was sitting and allowing myself to be consumed by my syndrome. Sure, I've had to get out of my comfort zone, and sure, I was scared. Just the thought of having to act scared me. But I would rather be scared than live with regret about not giving it my best shot. If I can choose to let procrastination consume me, surely I can choose to boot it out the door. We all choose what we want and do. I decided that I'd had enough. It was time for me to take control.

There is a difference between thinking about something and procrastinating. Thinking is merely regurgitating the same information over and over without any new input. I always state that you should not take any more than an evening or two to make up your mind on something once you have all the information in front of you. Any longer and you are simply making excuses. You either do something, or you don't. It's simple.

Do you know people who always say, "I've been thinking about …"?

One of the things I can't bear to hear is when friends come up to me and start their conversation with, "I've been thinking of starting a business. I've been thinking of …" Involuntarily, my brain switches off. To me, "I've been thinking" means "I am procrastinating."

Can you think of a time where procrastination actually helped you in a positive way?

What has procrastination brought you in your life so far? Since we all do it, surely there must be a very logical reason behind this madness? I am giving you a whole page to fill out everything the act of procrastination has brought for you in terms of positive results.

Now you have proof. You should have an empty page because this is what procrastination brings you—nothing. This is what procrastination contributes toward winning the game of life—*nothing*. In this book, we have just wasted a page; in the game of life that you're playing, a lot more is being wasted. Get Later Syndrome out of your life—*now*. Stop the madness. Grab a pen and write across the blank page, in bold letters: "TAKE CONTROL." Remember this act the next time you feel that you're getting consumed and retaliate by stepping up to action.

What one thing have you been procrastinating about lately?

_____

Write down what it would cost you to actually act on what you have been procrastinating about.

_____

Write down what is being wasted in your life because of procrastination.

_____

_____

"You may delay, but time will not."
—Benjamin Franklin, scientist, inventor, statesman, philosopher, musician, and economist

Procrastination costs you in many ways, and it's an expensive price to pay when you grasp the severity of it. People think that inaction doesn't have a hefty price to pay. I will suggest that the opposite is true. Think of the things you have not done. You will realize that you pay a lot more for not acting, for not taking a step, for not doing what you had to do. If you weigh up the risk of making a move against the risk of procrastinating, you'll see that making a move is the smart thing to do. Make the move. Speed things up to win your game of life. Do it *now*.

We all procrastinate in different aspects of our lives. Work on reducing your procrastination by a smidgen, and you'll achieve more. Winning the game of life is simple when you get your foot off the brakes and press on the accelerator. It's always easier to do what we already know, and many simply don't do what they already know. I am going to suggest that you know what you need to do to win the game of your life. You simply need to make a move. Put things to speed.

I've been asked many times, "What should I do with this situation? *How can I do this?* What do you recommend I do?"

After trying to answer friends' questions and thinking, "What would be the single most striking answer I could give?" Through observing, I came to realize the best answer.

When someone asks me for my thoughts on, say, how they can expand their business, move up the career ladder, excel in their sport, or work on making great personal connections, my reply these days is, "What do *you* think you should do to achieve the growth you are talking about? What do you think *you* must do?"

Their reply is usually an indication that they already know the answer but are simply not acting on what they know. People constantly ask questions to which they know the answers. Since they do not act on what they know, they feel that by asking the question, there might be a simpler, faster, or less painful way.

The fifteenth SECRET WEAPON mastered by those who are successful is that they *move on what they know.* Do what you already know you must do. If you consider yourself as having a top acumen, then make use of the knowledge you already possess. It'sfair to say that the place with the most ideas is the cemetery. Don't let your potential go to waste. *Make a move with what you know.*

GAME TIME

You're playing the game, and you're at a point where you can see the path ahead of you. You have never been down this path, and there's a lot of uncertainty. What if the place is booby-trapped? What if it's a smooth run? There are a lot of uncertainties. Standing there will not help you move ahead. Your character will not move until you make him or her move. You can take as long as you want; the character is waiting for your command. The end of the path will not come to you. The bottom line is you have to make a move and just handle the obstacles as they pop up, if they even pop up at all. When you are playing your game, if you decide to be lazy or take your time, your time will eventually expire. When your time expires, you're *gone*. You're better off making a move.

"Even if you're on the right track, you'll get run over if you just sit there."
—Will Rogers, cowboy, comedian, social commentator, performer, and actor

Here's what I see many people do: They're in their vehicle, and they're on the right highway to get where they want to go. Yet they're not getting to their destination because they've not started their engine and aren't pressing on the accelerator. The highway isn't going to move for you; you must move on the highway. I see so many people with potential who simply need to turn on the engine and get going. On top of that, it seems that they have their foot pressing on the brake and both hands on the hand brake—as if the car might move on its own. Many times, the fear holding people back is of the things they feel might pop up along the way.

How about you get moving and handle any obstacles as they come along, *if* they come along.

I have friends who always ask me, "What if this happens, Kevin? What if that happens?"

My answer is always, "How about we wait and see. *If* whatever you're concerned about happens, we'll think of something then." Thinking of reasons why we shouldn't get moving is absolute madness. You must *make a move on what you know* and figure things out along the way.

Successful people don't necessarily have the most knowledge; they are the ones who act on the knowledge they do have.

 What's the worst that could happen if you *made a move on what you know?*

_____

_____

What two things *must* you make a move on toward winning your game of life?

_____

_____

Take Home Message

Make a move on what you know. Time is very unforgiving. You might stay still, but the clock is always ticking.

16

*"People will not care how much you know,
until they know how much you care"*

— Anonymous

BECOME MESMERIZING AND COMPELLING

There are some people who are compelling. They are mesmerizing. They seem to have an aura about them.

What is it that gives them that edge? What makes them so compelling? How do some people do it?

Would you like to be compelling and mesmerizing too?

The first two things people think they need is to look good and be a good talker.

That could not be further from the truth.

Contrary to most people's belief, becoming compelling and mesmerizing has nothing to do with what you look like or even what you say.

List five people who are not exactly at the top of your friends list. You don't hate them, but you don't like them that much.

_____ _____ _____

_____ _____

I don't personally know you or the people you've written down, but I do know one thing. I know that they talk more about themselves than they want to know about you.

How many times have you come out of a conversation where you thought to yourself, "That person is really interesting"? Maybe you can recall a time when you thought you had the best conversation in the world with person X? Think of a few other occasions when you felt that way.

In almost every conversation that you have enjoyed, you were most likely the one who did the majority of the talking. The reason you enjoyed it and thought it was interesting was because you were the one talking. I can also assure you that the people with whom you had the conversation did not necessarily feel the same way. They might not tell you that though. This is where the majority of people are left wondering what they lack. They think they have tremendous rapport, they think have amazing conversations; yet they can never seem to get a date or make a sale. Why is that?

Let me give you a bit of background on human nature.

Human nature has it that we are all interested in ourselves. The mistake I see people make time and again is that they go on and on about all the things they've done, what their kids have done, or what they did during the weekend. Basically, they talk too much about themselves. People will only be interested to a point, and once you cross the one-minute mark continuously blabbering on about yourself, they'll shut off. The person hearing all this really isn't that interested. They are thinking about what movie they should go and watch or what they'll be having for dinner. They do all this whilst nodding and staring blankly at the noise you are making. Here you are thinking they are actually listening … They're not.

Cut the temptation to talk about yourself. The blunt truth is simply this: *They just don't care.* People are more interested in knowing how much you can care about them. People are interested if you can be of benefit to them. It's said that we are all tuned in to this very popular and international radio station. If you're not on this frequency, then the chances are you are not on a frequency at all. The favorite station common to everyone, in other words, the station you must often tune in to is WIIFM.

WIIFM stands for What's In It For Me? It sounds awful, and while some people will admit this fact, most will deny it. But that's exactly what's going through people's heads.

Once you manage to show that the person your're talking to what's in it for him or her, you will gain the other person's respect, and in return, he or she will genuinely want to know more about you. If people are always thinking about themselves, wouldn't it be wise to find out more about them and then be able to tailor-make your conversation, solution, or product to them? The more you accommodate the person you're communicating with, the more he or she will like you. When people like you, they trust you, and when they trust you, they will buy from you (whether it's buying you as a friend, a date, a business deal, a product, or a service). You are representing *you*, the brand, the product. This leads you to becoming more compelling and mesmerizing.

People are usually worried about what others might think. I'm sorry to break it to you, but most people don't bother to spend an extra minute thinking about you. They're too busy worrying about what others are thinking about them. Knowing this, you already have the heads up. You could be the talk of the town today and forgotten tomorrow, and that's the reality.

Ever wondered how some people just manage to seal the best deals? They seem to get the million-dollar contracts when the majority of people are struggling for thousand-dollar contracts. They seem to have passionate relationships when the majority of people are working hard only to face a breakup. They have the charisma most people talk about. They have an aura about them. It's because they perform the simplest yet most flattering act.

The most flattering thing you can do for anyone is to give him or her your full attention (this goes hand in hand with WIIFM). When you listen to someone, you are giving that person the utmost respect. Always focus on being present with the person you are communicating with. Always focus on being there. I'm not just talking about being there physically but being there 100 percent mentally. I used to call my brother up to chat and then whilst on the phone I would to check emails and let my mind wander to something else. It would drive my brother up the wall because I was not being present when I made the phone call. I never understood how painful it was until he started to do it to me. From that point on, we agreed that if we were to call one another, we would respect each other and be present on the phone, or there was no point calling. Needless to say, we have great conversations now and get straight to the point.

If you decide to listen to a friend, then spend the five, ten, twenty minutes truly being there and listening to your friend. People can sense when you're simply acting like you're listening while your mind is elsewhere, and they know when you're 100 percent truly there. Work on being 100 percent present wherever you are. This will very quickly set you apart from the rest. This single aspect will help you seal more deals, have better friendships, fuel passionate relationships, help you better communicate with the opposite sex, and much more. This weapon is very simple, yet it's one of the most powerful of THE SECRET WEAPONS. Successful people are masters of the sixteenth SECRET WEAPON: *actively listening.*

One afternoon, I was talking to a lady in her late forties whose kids had grown up. We were chatting about potentially doing business together, and from the word go, she seemed very closed and defensive. I knew that we would not move forward if she remained the way she was. After we'd chatted for a while, she still didn't seem to be at ease. Having *actively listened* and paid full attention to her, I realized that her kids were her pride and joy. I could see this from the spark in her eyes every time she mentioned one of her kids. I then asked questions about her kids and what they were doing with their lives? Instantly, she glowed and started chatting about them. She opened up from that point on, and we carried on having a very relaxed, warm, and successful talk, which went on for hours. Needless to say, we did business in the end. My business partner couldn't believe it. He had talked with this lady on numerous occasions and wondered why he couldn't get the same result. With a cheeky smile, I told him that his problem was just that—*he talked.*

"I know that you believe you understand what you think I said, but I'm not sure you realize that what you heard is not what I meant."
—Robert McCloskey, author and illustrator

A few years ago, if someone would had asked me to tell them the difference between hearing and listening, I would have told them that the two were synonymous. They're not. This is my own personal experience of hearing that I want to share with you. One night, my girlfriend comes home and starts telling me all about her day. I'm watching my favorite movie, and I'm engrossed in it because it's heading to the climax (or at least that is my excuse). I'm a guy after all and can only do one thing at a time. I am hearing my girlfriend make noises, but that is all her words are to me, noises. She realizes I'm not listening and, sure enough, the mood for the evening takes a plunge.

GAME TIME

You get to a point in the game where you're being instructed on what to do on the next level. You're being told of the things you must do, the items you must gather, the time frame you have. You're told everything you need to know in order to complete the next level. Now imagine if you decided to take a toilet break whilst the instructions were given on the screen. You come back, and you have missed the clues that were being shared on the screen by the computer character. You're on the next level, but you're left wondering why all your hard work isn't moving you forward. You thought listening to the tips on the screen wasn't important, and now you're stuck. You must listen with both ears, and that way, you will be able to conquer. The game is a lot easier if you listen and pay attention to the information that is given to you.

How many times have you been in that position with friends, business associates, or your spouse, where you were just in a different place mentally? You may have even been mentally alert, but you were so worried about talking that it didn't matter what the other person was saying. You wanted that person to grab a drink so that it could be your turn to start talking. I know I'm hitting a chord with most of you.

Let's try this out and really find out.

Think of a conversation or business meeting you had with someone in the last day or two.

Write down three things you know matter the most to this person:

1. _____

2. _____

3. _____

When you are not *actively listening*, the three things become a mission to write down. Nothing was sinking in because you were worried about what you were going to say next. If you have jotted down what truly matters to this person, then you are well on your way to mastering the art of *actively listening*.

Actively listening is a skill you must master. It is all about paying attention to what the other party is trying to convey, both in what he or she says and how he or she says it. By *actively listening*, you remember things about the people you talk with. It could be something to do with their work, family, or sports. Perhaps an associate told you that she was going to watch her son's game later in the day. If you were to meet that person in the next few days and ask, "Hey, by the way, how did your son's game go?" you'll not only hear the answer but see a smile beam from her face.

Get yourself a diary or create an electronic database on your computer. Use it to write notes about the meetings you have during the day. For example, in your meeting with John Smith, he mentioned that he had a surprise trip planned for his girlfriend to fly to Paris and pop the big question. After your meeting or at the end of your day, jot down a note in your diary about it. This serves as very strong ammunition for the next time you have a conversation with John Smith. People just love it if you remember something personal about them from a previous conversation because it shows that you were paying them full attention and were *interested* in them rather than in being *interesting*.

"A good listener is not only popular everywhere, but after a while he gets to know something."
—Wilson Mizner, playwright

I feel it's so important for everyone to know this because this single point can take your friendships, relationships, work or business to an *astonishing* level. It will boost you right through to the top. You will literally be mind boggled at the response you will get from people when you start to *actively listen*. People will sense something different about you, and the majority of them won't know what it is that's making you so mesmerizing. A few will pick up on your improved listening skills but the majority of people will be left wondering how you do it. You will be an enigma.

When you *actively listen*, you'll be able to understand what matters most to the person you're dealing with. You must not have the intention of selling your idea or product or be worried about what you'll get out of this conversation. You must genuinely spend time finding out more about the other person. You must drop your motive and be focused on truly getting to know the person. This will help you be genuine in understanding this person's needs. You never know, he or she could potentially become a lifetime friend. You have nothing to lose and everything to gain by being a great person to communicate with.

What is the easiest way to *actively listen*?

You don't even have to talk much or worry about having good things to say. All you have to do is learn to ask questions. Don't ask a question that will only give you a *yes* or *no* answer. Those are what we call closed-ended questions. You must ask open-ended questions—questions that help people open up to you and help you to see what matters the most to them. This will also help the conversation to flow instead of being filled with those awkward pauses that many of us have experienced. Ensure that your voice is sincere and not that of a person who's been trained to interrogate prisoners.

Examples of open-ended questions are:

How did you end up becoming a dentist?

Was it a passion for you, or did you fall in to it?

Tell me, what does studying for your PhD at Harvard involve?

What do you mean by that?

Does that concern you?

How was your holiday in Prague? How is Tom doing with his cricket? Have you looked at alternatives?

What are your thoughts about generating a second stream of income?

How do you think people are going to cope with the increase of mortgage interest rates?

How does that make you feel?

How do you see the future of your sport progressing? When was the first time you met your spouse?

What is it about your job/hobby/business/sport that brings you the greatest fulfillment?

(If you're still stuck trying to come up with more open-ended questions, you can get tons of examples by simply searching on Google for "examples of open-ended questions.")

You can ask many more open-ended questions to find out more about the person you're communicating with. You're not in any way interrogating people if your questions are genuine and caring. The next time you talk to someone, try to imagine that person as an onion and start gently peeling away layer by layer with your questions. You want to peel away and have the people you're conversing with bare their souls to you willingly so you can connect with them. Remember to do so without any ulterior motives. Always remember that this is about building great relationships with people.

When you pay attention and listen to people actively, you create a warm relationship. You create trust. When you're listening to someone, you're showing him or her respect and you're valuing him or her as a person. When you listen, people will like you, and the more you listen, the more they'll like you. If they like you, they'll trust you, and when they trust you, they'll listen to you. They will be open to new friendships, relationships, and partnerships with you.

You will be compelling and mesmerizing beyond your wildest imagination.

Have you been *actively listening* up until now in your life? (*Be honest.*)

_____

_____

List two areas where you can work on *actively listening?*

_____

_____

Take Home Message

When you find yourself talking a lot, just remember what the other person is thinking ...

WIIFM.

17

"If what you have done yesterday still looks big to you, you haven't done much today"

— Mikhail Gorbachev, (the last General Secretary of the Communist Party of the Soviet Union and the last head of state of the USSR)

THE ARTIST OF TODAY

You are young, you are old, you are black, you are white, you are tall, you are short, you are slim, or you are fat. Winning the game of life has nothing to do with what you are, where you have come from, how you look, or what you've done. Colonel Sanders was sixty-six when he made his successful recipe for Kentucky Fried Chicken. Thomas Edison failed ten thousand times before coming up with the light bulb. There are tons of stories out there that will illustrate the streak of failures (stumbling blocks) that successful people overcame before they became successful.

What matters is whether you do the right things today. Yesterday was just that—yesterday. It has no bearing on your life today. Yesterday is nothing. It can never be turned around, it cannot be repeated, and it can't dictate your future. Don't carry the baggage of yesterday into today. Tomorrow has not happened yet, so it is as good as nothing. Tomorrow is not a reality yet. So if yesterday is nothing, and tomorrow is nothing, then what can you control?

You can control *today*. Today is where you can make a better tomorrow. Today is when you can perform better than yesterday. Today is *everything*. Work to make today your best day. The seventeenth SECRET WEAPON mastered by those who are winning the game of life is that they *live and work in the now*. They learn from the past, plan for the future, but *live and work in the now*.

"I try to learn from the past, but I plan for the future by focusing exclusively on the present. That's where the fun is."
—Donald Trump, entrepreneur, television personality, and property tycoon)

Nothing matters except today and now. Your past doesn't dictate your future, and although you plan for the future, what will dictate your future is *now*.

When you don't have to worry about your past (or the future because it hasn't happened yet), all your focus can go on to the *now*, the present. The present is the gift you're given—a gift of choice, a gift of constantly being able to change your destiny. You must use the gift of today wisely. Those who do can be sure they'll win their game of life.

Today is when you learn from all the mistakes you've made in the past. Think of the times when you've learned the most. Was it when you got it right? Or was it when you got it wrong? We don't learn from the things we get right because, if we're not making mistakes, we're not growing. We learn from the mistakes we make, so take your mistakes in stride and enjoy the learning in whatever you do. Appreciate your mistakes.

Write down three lessons you've learned from making mistakes.

1. —————————————————————————————

2. —————————————————————————————

3. —————————————————————————————

The only real mistake is to make the same mistake over and over, without taking a stance and making a change. This is, unfortunately, where many go wrong.

Working on today will ensure that you'll have a better tomorrow.

It won't matter how hard you've worked in the past and it doesn't matter how long you've worked; what matters is today; what matters is *now*.

What are you doing right *now* to live the life of your dreams? To excel in your job, sport, or business? To have a great relationship?

"Live neither in the past nor in the future, but let each day's work absorb your entire energies and satisfy your wildest ambition."
—Sir William Osler

GAME TIME

You've reached level seventeen now. You've worked very hard to get here and have learned how to deal with many obstacles along the way. It could have taken you days to get to this point. But this is not the end of the game for you. Your battle continues, you must *constantly learn to grow*, and you must be willing to work just as hard if you want to finish this level. You cannot use the excuse that you worked so hard and for so long in the last sixteen levels that you don't need to work hard anymore. This is level seventeen, and it won't take care of itself. The last sixteen levels mean nothing anymore. You don't need to worry about the next level just yet. Your focus is to play your present level and get through it. You have no thoughts or concerns of the challenges from the past or the future ones that lie ahead. You have a plate full of challenges right now on this level. That is where your full concentration should be as a player. You are playing in the moment.

A blank or a painted canvas?

Most people base their lives on their past experiences. They let their past experiences be the painting on their canvas. They go into their present and future with the old painted canvas and then wonder why they're limited. They limit the potential of their lives to that one painting of the past. The painting on the canvas is a picture *you* have chosen to be there. Successful people paint on their canvas but then learn to start with a blank canvas at the beginning of every day. If they don't like the painted canvas from yesterday, then they leave it behind, but if they do, then they take it with them into the future.

The game of life gives us the opportunity of magic. We have a magic brush, and every day, we can use this brush to restore the paintings of the past (only the good ones) and erase others (the ones we don't like very much). If you have chosen to bring yesterday's painted canvas into today, and it's not a work of art, then how can you make way for a better painting on the canvas today?

Unless your canvas from yesterday is a piece of art, leave it behind. Every day is another opportunity to paint a better picture. You can't paint on your blank canvas if you are holding all the old worthless painted ones with both hands.

What is it that you want? A passionate relationship? To double your income? A great lifestyle? To compete at the top level in your sport? Whatever it is, you must paint that on your canvas. Your canvas is like the dream board I mentioned earlier on. Your mind's canvas must represent what you want. Go wild painting your masterpiece. There are no limits. The canvas in your mind is what you are aiming to materialize in your real world.

Nothing in your life's canvas is a mistake. Everything you have gone through so far is experience and has created who you are up until today. But you are in control. If your canvas needs changing, then you start painting again—starting today.

"The game should be played in the moment."
—Kevin Abdulrahman

What has your canvas looked like up until now? (*Be honest.*)

_____

_____

_____

List two things that you will paint on your canvas today to help you move toward winning your game of life?

_____

_____

 Take Home Message

Start every day with a blank canvas. You hold the brush, so create your *masterpiece* for today.

18

*"Not to act and make a move
is the biggest risk of all"*

– Kevin Abdulrahman

ALL OR NOTHING

This might not sit well with some of you. But at certain times in your life, you must take a calculated risk. No success comes without risk.

You must be a calculated risk taker. I don't mean that you should overanalyze things; rather, consider the variables and then take a leap of faith. What most people deem as risk is simply their lack of knowledge and understanding about a particular topic. Gain an understanding about any particular topic to reduce the perceived risk. Are you going to win every single time? Absolutely not. To think that way is absurd. All successful people have their wins and their losses. The key is to have bigger and more frequent wins than losses.

I have come across so many people who are living life by playing it safe. They're the biggest risk takers in my opinion, and their risk is not calculated. I remember meeting a gentleman who had been attending seminars. While chatting with him and asking a few questions, I found out that he'd attended hundreds of seminars over twenty years and many were about property. The shock came when he answered the question, "How many properties do you have?"

"'None," he replied. "I'm waiting for the right one. It's just too risky out there with the market constantly changing."

The right one? He had been through three property booms since his first seminar. It wouldn't have mattered what he had purchased, he would have easily quadrupled his money in twenty years. He could have bought a puddle anywhere around the world, and it would have outperformed his risk of inaction.

I know of people who have taken a couple of risks that didn't work out well for them, so then they stopped doing taking risks altogether. I went through that myself a few years ago, but then I realized I didn't want my past to dictate my future. Just because I made a loss in the past doesn't mean I will always make a loss. Just because I made a mistake in the past doesn't mean I will repeat that mistake. I wanted to give things a go so that I didn't live with the pain of regret. I would at least know that I gave it a shot.

How many people had the opportunity to buy into Google before it soared? How many people had the opportunity to buy a property before it doubled in value? How many people had the opportunity to buy into gold before it skyrocketed? How many people had the opportunity to invest in Microsoft but didn't? Those who did, based on doing the research and having the guts to act, benefited immensely. Successful people have mastered the eighteenth SECRET WEAPON: *taking calculated risk.*

"Risk is mostly nothing but a perception due to a lack of knowledge."
—Kevin Abdulrahman

GAME TIME

If you're playing a game against an army of "monsters," are you going to stand still and let them charge toward you, or are you better off to be in "attack mode" and fire at them? Simple. You stand still, you die. Standing still is not safe; it's the riskiest thing you could do because it brings you to imminent death. Fire through, and you will annihilate the monsters and move forward a level.

How many times have you played it safe? Discounting the one time that you were perhaps right in not making a move, cumulatively, can you honestly say that you are ahead in life due to playing it safe?

Yes ☐   No ☐

You could be the first, but I have yet to meet someone successful who has not taken a calculated risk at some point in their life.

When I talk about risk, I'm not talking about jumping off a cliff. I'm talking about the small things that get us out of our comfort zones. It could be applying for a job that you feel may stretch your abilities. It may be starting up a home-based business, something you have no idea about but that sounds like it could be a way for you to replace your salary. It could be competing in your sport on another level. It could be going to seminars and learning more about how to play the share market smartly. Have the guts to make a move and win your game of life.

I will use some numbers here to illustrate a point. This may have applied to you or to someone you know.

Imagine that it's five years ago, and you have access to twenty thousand dollars. I don't care if you don't have a dollar to your name or if twenty thousand dollars is a drop in the ocean to you. I believe that anyone can get twenty thousand dollars if they make it a must, one way or another.

Fast forward to the present and look at the table in fig. 4. Column A shows what most people did with their twenty thousand dollars because they wanted to avoid risk. They left their money in the bank. This is what doing so would look like if we assume the bank was paying 10 percent interest on your money (which they weren't, but we will go with that rate for this example).

Column B shows what would have happened if you had invested in a property and even applied the same rate of 10 percent increase (properties have done even more than that in most countries around the world in the last few years on average, cumulatively).

	Column A	Column B
	Money in the bank	**Money invested in a $200,000 property**
	Not wanting to risk	**$20,000 equates to a 10% deposit towards property so called risky**
$20,000	$20,000	$200,000
	$22,000	$220,000
	$24,200	$242,000
	$26,620	$266,200
	$29,282	$292,820
Year 5	$32,210	$322,102
Profit	$12,210	$122,102
	$32,210 - $20,000 initial investment	$322,102 - $200,000 (property price including initial investment)
Return on Investment	**61%**	**611%**

Fig. 4

A table that shows two very different investments of twenty thousand dollars.

Although this is very rough, and, no, I'm not taking many of the finer details into consideration. You will still come to the same conclusion, that the later return on investment is much higher.

This is only one of hundreds of examples. The number of people who play it safe far outweighs the number of people who take calculated risks. After all, from this worldwide and dominant example, who do you think ended up making the biggest loss and, in turn, the biggest realized risk? The person who thought he or she was playing it safe. I want to suggest that playing it safe is the biggest risk of all.

People play things safe, but they always lose in the long run. Yet if you risk, you have a chance to win. No one has ever become successful constantly playing it safe. There is always a period when some form of risk must be taken. If playing safe was the formula, then the majority of those playing would be successful. As we know, this is not the case.

Learn to not conform to what the masses want you to do. You will have to stand out at times and feel out of the social circle. But if you want to have a different result, you must do things differently.

Are you playing it safe in life? (*Be honest.*)

_____

_____

What two calculated risks can you take to help you win the game of life?

_____

_____

 Take Home Message

Always weigh up the true risks and rewards of both your actions and inactions.

"Reality is faced by everyone but only capitalized by some"

– Kevin Abdulrahman

19

GAME TIME

When the interest rates come down, I will buy a property.

When the economist predicts the next boom, I'll get into the share market.

When my finances are better, I'll get into a home-based business to so that I can generate a stream of income.

When people respect me, I'll respect them.

When my spouse takes care of me, then I'll take care of him or her. When this, when that—what a load of bull.

If you're waiting for everything to fall into place, for the timing to be just right for you to start something, then that moment will never happen. There will never be an ideal time. There is a time when you have to take action and, like I said earlier, successful people know that this time is *now*. Now is the time to do something. Now is the time to make a move. You don't have to get it perfect; you just need to get the ball rolling.

Many people, in their personal and professional lives, are just waiting for the perfect time to do something, and that perfect time never comes. If you don't take action now, you may very well never get going. Stop worrying about getting it right and just get a move on. Once you get things started, you can fine tune your mistakes as you go along. No matter how much you try to perfect something in theory, things do go wrong, and the best way to handle those stumbling blocks are by real life practice.

The time has come for you to play. It's game time. This is the most powerful secret weapon of all. Successful people have mastered the weapon of *taking action*. The difference that separates the winners from the rest is not in what they know, but in the action they take. *The Book* will be just another book if you do not apply THE SECRET WEAPONS in your life.

You probably know a lot of people who did well in the property market. It's not property itself; it's timing within the property game that made many people a heck of a lot of money. The same applied to gold. Those who took action and acquired knowledge about the investment easily doubled their money, compared to those who waited for the right time. Those who waited for the right time also missed Google's great run, which saw its share price grow more than eight times in a relatively short time period. Yet people are still sitting on the sidelines waiting for the perfect time.

The concept of talking versus walking

Of course, this would never be you. But how many times have you heard people say they're going to do something and never do it?

Most people trick themselves into thinking that, if they talk about doing something, it will happen.

News Break :

If that was the case, everyone would be successful.

There is no shortage of people talking the talk, but there is a huge shortage of people walking the walk. I may be harsh, but I want to drive my message home to you. Most people are delusional. They talk a lot about wanting to achieve great results, but talking is not enough.

When was the last time you decided to go to the gym?

When was the last time you said that you would start to live a healthier lifestyle?

When was the last time you were going to change your financial future by working smarter?

When was the last time you said that you would start a smart business to achieve the financial independence you want?

When was the last time you said you would train at a higher level in your sport?

When was the last time you said you would give before you take in your relationship?

We were at a seminar one day with friends, and for the lunch break, we thought we would go to this great burger outlet that makes the tastiest burgers. There were about twenty of us. This outlet provides customers with loyalty cards where, for every nine burgers you purchase, you can get the tenth one for free. By the time I parked my car, I was one of the last few to place my order. I thought to myself, "Hey, I said let's come to this burger place, and my friends have ordered fifteen or so burgers, fries, and drinks. Let me see if I can have a free meal based on their loyalty system."

The young guy behind the counter agreed with me, and I enjoyed a free meal. A couple of my friends turned around and told me, "Oh we thought of doing that when we first came in."

I could only reply, "Well, why didn't you?"

They got angry with me, but they were taking it out on the wrong person. They had the same opportunity as me yet didn't act. The difference was I simply acted on an opportunity. I won. A free burger wasn't the issue; the principle of acting on a thought was.

I could write a whole book on what people say they will do yet never take action on. When you don't do what you say you'll do, someone else will take your spot and enjoy the reward. How many times have you seen someone else do something and thought, "I thought of that a long time ago." Here's the deal: It doesn't matter who thinks of what first; what matters is who acts first.

GAME TIME

You are playing the game. Can you move forward with only good intentions? Are the weapons acquired any good if you're not going use them in battle? You need to put them into use in order to move up in the game. You will need to move your controller for your character to charge ahead.

You be the judge for yourself. You are where you are in life because of the actions you have taken. Where are you in life?

Should you be taking more action?

One of your action steps should be to go over the dream life you wrote about in the previous chapter. Write down ten action steps you must take to move toward winning the game of life.

_____

_____

_____

_____

_____

_____

_____

_____

_____

Another *action* step you must take is to reread this book in one month. You'll be able to see your progress, and you'll also learn a stack of new information purely from being in a different place.

The years you have lived so far should be enough of an indication of what opportunities you've seized or missed based on whether you have taken action or not.

The Book and all THE SECRET WEAPONS shared here are only as good as the person who will put them to use. There are two types of people in this world—those who will read every book under the sun and spend all their lives continuously learning and searching but with no signs of action and those who will act on what they learn and have the guts to make mistakes. They have the guts to learn and do—to practice and master THE SECRET WEAPONS. They have the guts to go after their dreams.

I have shared with you THE SECRET WEAPONS that have helped me and other successful people win the game of life. But the choice, whether you'll adapt them into your life, will remain yours.

Mastering THE SECRET WEAPONS will only come from action—something only you *must* decide to do.

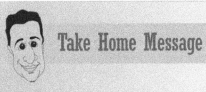

Take Home Message

Talk is cheap. Value is measured not by what a person says but by what he or she acts upon.

Before you start your journey toward winning the game of life, I want you to pick one thing you would like to achieve. It could be a financial goal, a personal goal. Whatever it may be, write:

I am committed to achieving my goal of _____

_____

_____

_____

Write down twenty-five things you'll do once you've achieved your goal.

(For example, you might write, "The twenty-five things I will do once I have started to make two thousand dollars a week.)

The twenty-five things I will do once I achieve _____

_____ are

1. _____

2. _____

3. _____

4. _____

5. _____

6. _____

7. _____

8. _____

9. _____

10. _____

11. _____

12. _____

13. _____

14. _____

15. _____

16. _____

17. _____

18. _____

19. _____

20. _____

21. _____

22. _____

23. _____

24. _____

25. _____

Review this page and tick off each item as you accomplish your goal. Share it with the people who will hold you accountable.

I look forward to hearing your success stories (Submit your story on our Website, located at www.thisisTHEBOOK.com or email your success story to info@KevinAbdulrahman.com)

CONGRATULATIONS

You have come to the end of *The Book*, but you've just got to the beginning of your new life.

It's time.

Will information alone be the key to you winning the game of life?

The sad but real truth is no.

I'll keep this short because you need to get down to business

I ask you to take each weapon on board and put all of them into action in whatever game you're playing in life. If what you've learned is the equivalent of acquiring a Ferrari, I ask you to insert the key, turn on the ignition, and press down on the accelerator. There is no point owning a beautiful super car and having it sit in the garage gathering dust. For the ladies, what would be the point of buying a beautiful dress and never wearing it?

The time has come. Take all your energy and start applying THE SECRET WEAPONS to win the game of your life. The road you travel will be one of great adventure, and you will always be in control of what road you take. It will feel uncomfortable at first, but so does trying to take your first few baby steps, trying to tie your shoelaces the first few times, and learning to drive. When was the last time you thought about walking? You don't. It's simply something you mastered and do on a subconscious level. By mastering these weapons, you can make it a habit to constantly use them. One day, you will be called *lucky*. And just like not having to think of walking, you too will end up winning the game of life.

I take my hat off to those of you who will go out and make a difference in your own lives.

Share your success with the world on www.thisisTHEBOOK.com.

May you win the game of your life

Cheers,

Kevin Abdulrahman 'The Man Inspiring Millions'

SMART NOTES

SMART NOTES

SMART NOTES

SMART NOTES

SMART NOTES

SMART NOTES

SMART NOTES

SMART NOTES

SMART NOTES

SMART NOTES

To reach
the Author

Media enquiries

For all media inquiries, publicity photos, interview questions, or articles to reprint, please make your request to media@KevinAbdulrahman.com

General inquiries:

For all general inquiries and how you can have Kevin Abdulrahman speak to your group, please make your request to info@KevinAbdulrahman.com

Book Kevin Abdulrahman, 'The Man Inspiring Millions'

Kevin Abdulrahman Continues to impact the lives of people from all around the world. He is committed to spending time with the people he cares about the most. his free time, Kevin Abdulrahman is available for international group talks, trainings, mentoring, coaching and key-note speaking engagements. If you want real impact; no nonsense; and a straight-to-the-point approach, then you want Kevin Abdulrahman to be in front of your group.

For further information, email info@KevinAbdulrahman.com

Please provide us with information such as the size of your group, location, topics you want to be discussed, areas you want to boost, and your budget.

Stay in Touch

We want to hear your success story, so stay in touch and let us know how you are doing. You can do so by going on www.thisisTHEBOOK.com

We are in the process of compiling several books—one of which will be a compilation of people achieving great success in any aspect of their lives. If you would like to be considered to have a chapter in *The Book* on today's success stories (title to be confirmed) then do submit it www.thisisTHEBOOK.com

Ensure you give us all your details correctly so we can contact you should you qualify.

Bulk Purchases for Your TEAM

If you would like friends, family, or business associates to learn and excel from reading *The Book*, we can look at doing a bulk price for you.

Email us at info@thisisthebook.com and inform us of what you would like to do. We will be happy to help.

Attend a Lifestyle Millionaire Workshop

We are in the process of putting together an exclusive, five-day seminar in an exotic location. Details of this seminar are still under wraps, but we can share with you that it will be limited to only fifty people. This is not for everyone, as you will need to be of a certain caliber and have achieved some milestones. It will require that you contribute a minimum of US $15,000, take one week off whatever you are doing, and seriously commit to taking action with what you learn.

We'll discuss THE SECRET WEAPONS from *The Book* amongst many other things that will help attendees break through to amazing heights. You will hear from a number of speakers who are successful within their own rights. The workshop will incorporate some amazing, fun outdoor activities, along with serious mingling of people who are in the same headspace.

What you will come out with will see you potentially double, triple, or quadruple your income

To express your interest, email us at workshop@thisisTHEBOOK.com

Fill in your details. When a date is confirmed, you'll be kept informed via email and a phone call from one of our staff.

Donations Made for Every Book that is Purchased from thisisTHEBOOK.com

We believe in giving to those less fortunate than ourselves. Because of that, we are making a commitment to raise one million dollars from the continuous sale of *The Book* through www.thisisTHEBOOK.com I have set a big goal because I want to make a big difference.

But I can't do it on my own. *I need your help*.

If you would like to be part of my vision to give back, and if you've have found *The Book* to be of great value, do let others know where to get a copy; in the process, they will grow, and you'll be part of creating a positive wave.

Together, we can make a difference in this world. Our initial target is to raise one

million dollars. Some have laughed at us for our silly expectation, but we believe that a few people with the same vision can not only hit this target but surpass it. The sky is the limit with what we can give back.

All you have to do is tell people who you feel could benefit from reading *The Book*, and with every purchase they make from www.thisisTHEBOOK.com one dollar will be going toward charity.

I thank you in advance for sharing our vision to give back to this beautiful world that we live in.

BUY A SHARE OF THE FUTURE IN YOUR COMMUNITY

These certificates make great holiday, graduation and birthday gifts that can be personalized with the recipient's name. The cost of one S.H.A.R.E. or one square foot is $54.17. The personalized certificate is suitable for framing and will state the number of shares purchased and the amount of each share, as well as the recipient's name. The home that you participate in "building" will last for many years and will continue to grow in value.

Here is a sample SHARE certificate:

YES, I WOULD LIKE TO HELP!

*I support the work that Habitat for Humanity does and I want to be part of the excitement! As a donor, I will receive periodic updates on your construction activities but, more importantly, I know my gift will help a family in our community realize the dream of homeownership. **I would like to SHARE in your efforts against substandard housing in my community!** (Please print below)*

PLEASE SEND ME _____ SHARES at $54.17 EACH = $ $_____

In Honor Of: _____

Occasion: (Circle One)   HOLIDAY   BIRTHDAY   ANNIVERSARY

     OTHER: _____

Address of Recipient: _____

Gift From: _____ *Donor Address:* _____

Donor Email: _____

I AM ENCLOSING A CHECK FOR $ $_____ PAYABLE TO HABITAT FOR HUMANITY <u>OR</u> PLEASE CHARGE MY VISA OR MASTERCARD *(CIRCLE ONE)*

Card Number _____ Expiration Date: _____

Name as it appears on Credit Card _____ Charge Amount $ _____

Signature _____

Billing Address _____

Telephone # Day _____ Eve _____

PLEASE NOTE: Your contribution is tax-deductible to the fullest extent allowed by law.
Habitat for Humanity • P.O. Box 1443 • Newport News, VA 23601 • 757-596-5553
www.HelpHabitatforHumanity.org

Printed in the USA
CPSIA information can be obtained
at www.ICGtesting.com
JSHW082202140824
68134JS00014B/372